ROYAL DOULTON SERIES WARE

Design by Paul Sharp
Photography by Prudence Cuming Associates
Printed and bound in Great Britain by
Robert Stockwell Limited, London SE1
Produced by Paul Atterbury
Published and distributed by Richard Dennis
144 Kensington Church Street, London W8

ISBN 0 903685 07 8

Acknowledgements

I am deeply indebted to Royal Doulton Tableware
Limited for permission to reproduce material from
their archives, and for their generous cooperation
in the preparation of this book.
   I should like to thank the author, Louise
Irvine, for her particular dedication and
expertise, and Jill Rumsey who undertook much
of the historical and literary research.
   Additional thanks are due to the Dickens House
Museum, Desmond Eyles, Charles Gibbs-Smith,
John Jenkins, Jocelyn Lukins, Stephen Nunn,
Ian and Rita Smythe and Caroline Wilkinson

RD
August 1980

Contents

Top to bottom, left to right: Dickens jug, Canterbury Pilgrims jug, Bradley jug, Burns vase, Rip van Winkle jug, Sir Roger de Coverley vase, Dickens candlestick, Jackdaw of Rheims jug, Historic England coffee pot, Shakespeare jug, Eglington Tournament jug, Bateman tankard, Old English Inns teapot, Under the Greenwood Tree jug

Royal Doulton Series Ware

Series ware was the brainwave of Charles J. Noke who joined Doulton at Burslem in 1889 and later became Art Director. He devised a scheme for employing a vast number of standard blank shapes including rack plates or plaques, vases, trays, jugs and tea sets and decorating them with a wealth of popular imagery. 'Novelty Art Wares' or 'Fancy Lines', as they were originally called, could 'adorn yet serve some useful purpose' according to a contemporary advertising brochure and also 'solved the problem of the inexpensive small gift'. The assortment of items was designed to suit every taste and need, colour schemes and decorative borders were varied for wider appeal and often there was a choice of an earthenware or bone china body. A series might depict two or three scenes or around twenty and the customer was encouraged, much as the collector is today, to add to his collection until he had the complete set.

A few of the Series ware subjects were inherited from the Pinder Bourne range and continued in production for some time after Doulton took over that factory in 1882. One of the earliest recorded depicts ancient Greek chariot races and is known as the *Isthmian Games*. Scenes of dancing girls, playing children and subjects suitable for the nursery were also popular at this early period.

Left C. J. Noke   *Right* One of the decorating shops at the Burslem factory, c1910

From 1899 onwards however, C. J. Noke's fertile imagination was at work developing new ideas for Series ware. Each year a succession of designs went into production. Characters from legend and song or from literature and history were the inspiration for many patterns. Popular sports and pastimes such as hunting, golfing, fishing and motoring were also depicted on a variety of wares. Nostalgic images of 'Olde Worlde' England and other countries were continual favourites as were studies of animals and flowers. Many designs were conceived specially for children and these nursery wares form a charming aspect of Series ware collecting. Important events were often commemorated on Doulton Series ware creating yet another interesting collecting category. The list is endless and repeatedly demonstrates Noke's instinctive gift for what would have popular appeal.

Noke himself was responsible for many of the original drawings and sometimes the series bears his facsimile signature. A skilled team of artists supported him in this work but few of them were credited on the ware. William Edmund Grace worked on the Series ware ranges from 1902 until 1959, whilst Walter Nunn is recognised for his work on the *Old London* series and many others. Arthur Eaton, George Holdcroft, Stanley Woodman, Cecil Jack Noke, Harry Tittensor and Leonard Langley are also recorded as having played major roles in the development of this aspect of Doulton production. Sometimes studies from these artists' personal sketchbooks were developed into Series ware patterns. Most of the designs, however, reflect the influence of contemporary book illustrators or cartoonists. Noke's drawings for the *Dickens* series for example are very closely based on the work of 'Kyd' (Joseph Clayton Clark), one of the celebrated illustrators of Dickens' works.

A variety of printing techniques created the diverse Series ware styles. Transfer printing from engraved plates and lithography were often used in conjunction with hand colouring, a process known in the industry as 'print and tint'. Block printing and silk-screening were employed for denser, more colourful images. A photographic process was also developed to record famous views, characters and various other scenes on rack plates.

The finished effect varied with the colour of the glaze, sometimes pale yellow or ivory which rendered a natural colour scheme or else a dark yellow glaze known as *Holbein* which created a rich glowing effect. Sometimes more unusual effects were used such as *Titanian* glaze with its mottled lustrous blue-green colouring, or *Celadon* glaze, a subtle green reminiscent of Chinese precedents of the same name.

Whieldon ware, a rather coarse earthenware with slip-painted detail, sometimes featured Series ware designs, but refined earthenware or bone china were the most common bodies employed. English translucent china, invented by Doulton in 1967, was used for the few remaining rack plate designs.

World War II interrupted the production of Series ware and, in its aftermath, 'fancy lines' no longer enjoyed their former popularity. The range of series gradually dwindled in the 'fifties and by the 'sixties it was predominantly rack plates featuring flora or fauna or photographic views which remained in production.

In the last decade, however, there has been a revival of decorative plate production at Royal Doulton. The *Collectors International* plates—a series depicting paintings by well-known artists—made their appearance in 1973 and have enjoyed growing popularity amongst American collectors. *Valentines Day Plates* and *Christmas Plates*, with nostalgic impressions of past festivities have been issued annually since 1976 and 1977 respectively and continue to be favourites amongst plate collectors.

Whether it be contemporary display plates or out of production 'fancy lines', Doulton Series ware offers plenty of scope for a varied and fascinating collection. Some collectors pursue a particular theme such as *Dickens* subjects or hunting scenes and try to find as many different items as possible. The permutations of scenes and shapes seem endless and collectors might expect to find over fifty items in some of the major series. Some collections are formed exclusively of rack plates accumulated for their interesting subject matter or sometimes for aesthetic reasons alone. Whatever their tastes, collectors should find something to satisfy them in the Doulton Series ware range.

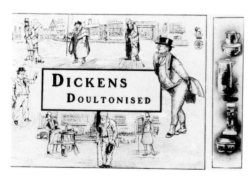 

Doulton advertising postcards for Series ware, c1912

Introduction to Volume 1

This volume is the first of several on the subject of Series wares and related items. It deals with three categories, Literature, Popular Illustrators and Historical Characters and Events. Forthcoming volumes will include 'Olde Worlde' imagery, flora and fauna, photographic scenes, nursery and commemorative wares.

Most of the subject matter in volume 1 reflects the personal interests of C. J. Noke. An avid reader in his spare time, he discovered in many of his favourite novels, plays and poems ideal characters for immortalising in ceramic. Shakespeare, the most celebrated writer in the English language, was an obvious first choice. In 1899 twelve incidents from seven of his plays formed the first of many *Shakespeare* series.

Dickens was undoubtedly Noke's first love and provided him with the inspiration for a remarkable range of characters in appropriate settings which drew high praise from Dickens' son. 'I think the conception of the figures, the colouring and the general execution of the whole work most admirable and not easily to be surpassed. I feel quite sure this ware will be much approved and sought after by all readers and lovers of my father's works'.

'Dickens Doultonised' (the original name for the series) was, and still is, one of the most popular series but Noke and his artists did not neglect other literary masters, however obscure. Robert Burns, Geoffrey Chaucer, Laurence Sterne, Henry Longfellow, Jonathan Swift and many others all had their characters perpetuated on Doulton Series ware.

Noke did not rely solely on the talents within the Doulton studios to increase and popularise the Series ware range, he also capitalised on the reputation of famous illustrators and cartoonists. In 1900 Doulton acquired the rights to reproduce the work of the American illustrator Charles Dana Gibson and the 'Gibson Girl' plates became one of their best selling lines. Around the same time, the drawings of fellow countryman Will Bradley appeared on a wide variety of items. C. J. Noke quickly followed these successes by adding to the range the striking cat cartoons of David Souter, the anthropomorphic dogs of Cecil Aldin and the satirical studies of Henry Mayo Bateman. Surprisingly Doulton were one of the few potteries to avail themselves of these humorous images ideally suited to ceramics in their simplicity and economy of line.

Noke again demonstrated his astute awareness of popular taste when he romanticised our heritage on Series ware. Picturesque views of castles, churches, stately homes and old inns decorated a variety of items. He introduced the pomp and ceremony of historical incidents, and paid tribute to former naval heroes and their exploits. Topical events were also celebrated on china, for example the first air race held at Rheims and World War I.

Named monuments and specific historical events and characters will appear in this volume. Scenes which are historical in feeling but which do not refer to any particular episode in the past will be found in the future volume containing 'Olde Worlde' subjects. Any series not included in this volume will almost certainly appear in a subsequent volume.

Don Quixote. Rack plate C1
(See page 32)

Top bot bottom, left to right: Aeronautical Scenes spittoon, Shakespeare vase, Authors and Inns jug, Bayeux Tapestry jug, Rip van Winkle jug, Under the Greenwood Tree beaker, Dickens loving cup, Under the Greenwood Tree jug, Aldin teapot, Dickens jug, Diversions of Uncle Toby jug, Under the Greenwood Tree teapot, Bradley vase

Rack plates. *Top to bottom, left to right:* Caldecott, Omar Khayyam, Don Quixote, Shakespeare, St George, Hiawatha, Diversions of Uncle Toby, Castles and Churches, Historic England, Jansson, Under the Greenwood Tree, Jackdaw of Rheims

How to use this book

The series in this volume are divided into three appropriate sections: Literature, Popular Illustrators, and Historical Characters and Events. The *Aldin* series, for example, will be found in the Popular Illustrators section, whilst *Famous Sailing Ships* will be located in the Historical section.

Each series is listed alphabetically within the section under its correct title if known, otherwise its most common title. Where an author's name is the title of the series it is the surname which denotes its alphabetical order, for example, William Shakespeare is entered under S. When the exact title is not known the series can be located with reference to the index which lists names of characters featured or quotations and inscriptions.

SERIES DETAILS
After some brief background details about the characters and events depicted, information on each series is entered under several headings for easy reference.

SCENES OR TITLES
In each series the number of different scenes depicted can range from one to around twenty. When the exact title of the scene has been recorded, quotation marks are used. Otherwise a description of the image is given to aid identification.

CHARACTERS
Some series such as *Souter* or *Izaak Walton* have this additional heading where all the different figure or animal poses recorded in that series are described.

PATTERN NUMBERS
All the D or E numbers so far recorded for each series are listed together. Sometimes one pattern number can refer to the entire series, for example, D2873 is the *Bayeux Tapestry* series. In this case the pattern number can be a useful aid for tracing more items in the series. More often, however, each series has several different pattern numbers which denote the use of varying colourways, borders or shapes. The date of introduction of each design is indicated by the pattern number. See the *Date Guide* on p. 102.

BORDERS
When a pattern was produced with more than one border, the variations are listed under this heading. For example, *Arabian Nights* has three borders so far recorded: Japanese, trailing vine and plain red band. Wherever possible border variants have been illustrated.

COLOURWAYS
The majority of Doulton series ware decoration is polychrome and in this case no specific reference is made to colour. However, any other variations are listed, such as blue and white, sepia, or green and white. When unusual glaze effects or bodies are recorded these are also listed, for example Holbein glaze, Whieldon ware, or Celadon ware.

SHAPES
An enormous variety of shapes were used in the Series ware range. Under this heading an indication is given of the extent of each series and the types of shapes employed for that pattern. By consulting the *Shape Guide* on p. 104 collectors may become familiar with the most common vase numbers and shape names. Many items are not illustrated in the shape guide, in particular the diverse bone china shapes and specially moulded items.

DATES
The introduction and withdrawal dates are given when they are recorded. Pattern numbers are a useful guide to dating in conjunction with the *Pattern and Code Numbers Guide* (*Date Guide*) on p. 101.

DESIGNERS
The designer's name is given when it is known but this is rarely the case.

SPECIAL BACKSTAMP

In addition to the Royal Doulton trademark some series had their own specially designed backstamp. Examples of some of the more interesting are given below.

The information for this book has been gleaned from surviving Doulton pattern books and from major collections. Although this is the most comprehensive study on Series ware produced so far it cannot claim to be complete. Some of Doulton's records are missing and with them, no doubt, further details of Series ware scenes, pattern numbers, glaze effects and so on. It is hoped that collectors will inform us of any additional material they discover in order that future studies will be more complete.

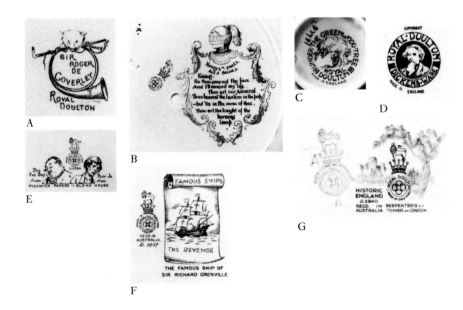

Series ware backstamps: A Special backstamp for Sir Roger de Coverley wares, c1908. B Special backstamp for Shakespeare wares, factory mark and date code for 1908. C Special backstamp for Under the Greenwood Tree wares, c1915. D Special backstamp for Dickens wares, c1912. E Special backstamp for Dickens wares, c1930. F Special backstamp for Famous Ships wares, 1940. G Special backstamp for Historic England wares, factory A mark and registration mark, c1945

Arabian Nights. *Above* 1; *below* 2

Arabian Nights. *Left to right, above* 5, 8; *below* 8, 4, 2

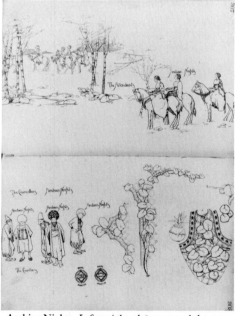

Arabian Nights, 8

Arabian Nights. *Left to right, above* 12, 11; *below* 10, border details and special backstamp

Subjects from Literature

Arabian Nights

Also known as *The Thousand and One Nights* this series of stories is largely of Persian origin (although written in Arabic). The first European translation was in French, 1704–17. English translations include Burton's 16 volumes, 1885–8. The stories are linked by Scheherezade who keeps her husband in suspense by telling stories for 1001 nights thus avoiding death, the fate of previous wives. In one story, Ali Baba takes the Forty Thieves' treasure and is saved from their revenge when Morgiana, his slave, pours boiling oil over them.

Ali Baba and the Forty Thieves
SCENES/TITLES
1 Ali Baba and the thieves
2 Ali Baba at the cave, 'Open Sesame'
3 Ali Baba and the treasure
4 Ali Baba's return
5 Morgiana pouring oil 'She poured into each jar in turn a sufficient quantity of boiling oil'
6 Morgiana and Ali Baba

The Magic Horse
7 'It was in vain that all the wisest physicians in the country were called into consultation'

General Themes
8 'Preparing for the Feast'
9 'The Arrival of the Unknown Princess'
10 'The Councillors'
11 'The Attendants'
12 'The Courtiers'
13 Character reading 'The Arabian Nights'

PATTERN NUMBERS
D.3198, D3323, D3420.

BORDERS
Japanese, plain red band, trailing vine.

SHAPES
Rack plates, Corinth teapot, Lennox flower pot, spittoon, tobacco jars, vase numbers 7352, jugs (not in shape guide).

DATES
This series was introduced in 1909 and expanded with new border patterns in 1911. It appears to have been totally withdrawn in 1928.

SPECIAL BACKSTAMP

Arabian Nights. Rack plates, *left to right*, 7 with Japanese border, 8 and 9 with trailing vine border

Beggar's Opera

The Beggar's Opera written by John Gay tells the story of the dashing highwayman Captain MacHeath and his love for two women Polly Peachum, an innkeeper's daughter and Lucy Lockit, a jail warden's daughter. The opera was first performed in 1728 and was revived in 1920 at the Lyric Theatre, Hammersmith. Following the revival Doulton produced a range of figures based on these characters.

SCENES/TITLES
Characters from the Beggar's Opera.

PATTERN NUMBERS
Not recorded.

SHAPES
Rack plate.

DATES
This design was featured in the pattern book of 1936. It is not known how long it was in production.

Beggars Opera characters

Robert Burns

Robert Burns (1759–96) is Scotland's best-known poet. A cotter's son, educated by his father, Burns' writings in the Scots dialect were an immediate success. His meeting with Captain Grose led to his writing 'Tam O'Shanter' for Grose's book—*Antiquities in Scotland* and making Tam the subject of both poem and song. Two of Burns' most famous works are the poem, 'A Cotter's Saturday Night' and the song 'Auld Lang Syne'.

A

SCENES/TITLES
1 'Here's a health to them thats awa'.

CHARACTERS
1 Scotsman in tammy holding jug and glass.
2 Scotsman with glass aloft and pipe on table.
3 Scotsman with glass aloft.

PATTERN NUMBERS
D3368

BORDER
Thistle or no border.

COLOURWAYS
Polychrome, Holbein glaze.

SHAPES
Rack plates, Stafford dessert plate, Lennox flower bowl, self-pouring teapot.

DATES
These designs were introduced in 1910 and withdrawn around 1924.

B Bobbie Burns
SCENES/TITLES
1 *'The Cotters Saturday Night,*
They round the ingle form a circle wide,
The big ha bible ance his father's pride'.
2 '*A Cottage Home*
His clean hearth stane his thrifty wifie's smile
The lisping infant prattling on his knee'.
3 '*Captain Grose*
Ken ye ought o' Captain Grose I go ago
If he's among friends or foes Iram, coram dago'.
4 '*Green grow the rushes o*
The sweetest hours that e'er I spend are spent among the lassies o'.

Burns. *Above* A2, *centre* A1, *below* A3

Burns. *Left to right, above* B2, B3, B8, *centre* B4 with laurel leaf border, B5, *below* B6, *bottom* B1

Burns. Rack plates, *left to right* B5, B2, B4 with laurel leaf border

5 '*I hae a wife*
I hae a wife o' my ain
I'll partake wi naebody
I'll tak cuckold frae nane
I'll gie cuckold to naebody'.
6 '*Halloween*
And many lads and lassies fates
Are there that night decided'.
7 'Here's a health to Charlie
The chief o' the clan'. (Two versions).
8 '*Tam O' Shanter*
Kings may be blest but Tam was glorious
O'er all the ills o' life victorious'.
9 'John Anderson my Jo, John

We clamb the hill the gither'.
10 'What can a young lassie do wi an auld man?
He is always compleenin frae morning to e'enin'.

PATTERN NUMBERS
D3368, D3385, D4419, E8289.

BORDERS
Laurel leaf or no border.

SHAPES
Rack plates, Leeds square and round fruit

Rack plates. *Top to bottom, left to right:* Shakespeare, Famous Sailing Ships, Robert Burns, Gallant Fishers, Old English Inns, Bayeux Tapestry

Page from a Doulton pattern book, showing a Shakespeare design for a rack plate

Burns. Rack plates, *left to right* B3, A2 with thistle border, B7

"Burns' Subjects." D 4419.

"Burns' Subjects." D 4419.

Selection of Burns ware (catalogue page)

dishes, Lennox flower bowl, Cecil coffee service, Clive tea service, Pelican trinket set, Pitt jugs, porridge plate, oatmeal saucer, fruit saucer, Rex mug, round salad bowl, Napier, New Rim, 89 and Ancestor ashtrays, sandwich tray, Harlech teacup and saucer, Corinth tea service.
Vase numbers 7023, 7346, 7348, 7384, 7385, 7387, 7397, 7493, 7531, 7532, 7538A and B.

DATES
The series was first introduced in 1910 and remained in production until 1951 during which time there were changes in border designs and additions and deletions of many items.

C Burns portrait
SCENES/TITLES
1 Bust of Burns with ploughhorses behind.
2 Bust of Burns with his cottage behind.

PATTERN NUMBERS
D3391, D3392, D3397, D3688, D6344, TC1040.

BORDERS
Pierced, thistle, and images of his characters.

COLOURWAYS
Polychrome, green and white, blue and white.

SHAPES
Rack plates.

DATES
This design was introduced in 1911 in various colourways. It was redrawn in 1950 with modifications in style and border. This version remained in production until 1968 when it was replaced by the translucent china version. The china version was withdrawn in 1975.

Canterbury Pilgrims

Written in verse by Geoffrey Chaucer (c1340–1400), The Canterbury Tales tell of twenty-nine pilgrims who meet at the Tabard Inn, Southwark, London, before journeying to Canterbury to visit the tomb of the martyr Thomas à Becket. They entertain each other on the journey by exchanging tales. The group includes a 'chivalrous' knight and his son, 'a lad of fire'; a tender-hearted prioress; five 'worthy' burgesses and a widow of Bath who 'liked to laugh and chat'.

SCENES/TITLES
1 The scene of the martyrdom
2 Geoffrey Chaucer portrait

CHARACTERS
1 Chaucer
2 The pipe player
3 Group of three characters (the three priests?)
4 Group of five characters including the Widow of Bath, the Friar and the Monk
5 Group of five characters including the Franklin?, the Pardoner and drinking man
6 Group of six characters including the Bailiff and the Prioress
7 Group of eight characters including the Squire, the Yeoman and the Knight
Note Various combinations of these groups were used on different items sometimes in conjunction with one or both of the scenes above.

PATTERN NUMBERS
D3188.

BORDER
Lion and rose.

Burns. Rack plates, *left to right* C2, C1

Canterbury Pilgrims. *Left to right, above* 7, 4, *centre* 6, 3, *below* 2, 1, 5

Canterbury Pilgrims. *Left to right,* rack plate 1, 7, jug 4, rack plate 5, 3, jug with Chaucer portrait

SHAPES
Rack plates, Concord jug, Dame tea service,
candlestick 7277, Loving cup 7352, Durham
fern pot, round salad bowl.

DATES
This series was in production from 1909 until
around 1933.

Dickens

The son of a government clerk, Charles Dickens (1812–70) underwent in early life experiences of poverty similar to those of David Copperfield. His first book, *Pickwick Papers*, was issued in twenty monthly parts from April 1836. His books are notable for their detail and accuracy with regard to everyday Victorian life. C. J. Noke was a great admirer of Dickens, and so Doulton featured a wide range of his characters, listed here according to the novel in which they appear. Many examples of Dickens ware carry Noke's signature, but in fact many of the designs were based closely on the Dickens characters drawn by the illustrator Joseph Clayton Clark, or 'Kyd' as he was known.

Bleak House: The pious and elegant *Mr. Chadband*; and *Jo* the crossing sweeper, chivvied to death by the police.
The Chimes: (*Toby*) *Trotty Veck*, who has visions, under the influence of church bells and a bowl of tripe, of his daughter's misfortunes.
Martin Chuzzlewit: His good-humoured servant *Mark Tapley*; *Pecksniff* and his daughters *Charity* and *Mercy*; his loyal assistant *Tom Pinch* and *Sairey Gamp*, the disreputable nurse.
David Copperfield: The 'umble' *Uriah Heep*; *Barkis*, the carrier, *Old Peggotty*, and the impecunious *Mr. Micawber* who finally becomes a colonial magistrate.
Dombey and Son: *Mr. Toots*, the innocent and humble admirer of Dombey's daughter; *Captain Cuttle*, a genial old sea-captain.
Nicholas Nickleby: *Squeers*, the cruel headmaster, *Newman Noggs* and *Mr Mantalini* who ruined his wife a fashionable dressmaker.
Old Curiosity Shop: *Dick Swiveller* who works for *Quilp*, who ruined *Little Nell's* grandfather.
Pickwick Papers: Together with *Pickwick*, *Augustus Snodgrass*, *Tracy Tupman* and *Nathaniel Winkle* were the Corresponding Members of the Pickwick Club, the expenses for their travels being paid by the Club; *Tony Weller* the coachman, Pickwick's resourceful servant *Sam Weller*, his landlady, *Mrs. Bardell* and her lawyer *Mr. Dodson* and counsel *Buzfuz*, the rascally actor *Alfred Jingle* and the cheery *Fat Boy* are also featured.
Barnaby Rudge: *Barnaby Rudge*, who is always accompanied by his raven.

The Tale of Two Cities: *Sydney Carton*, a barrister who takes his friend's place on the French guillotine.
Oliver Twist: *Oliver Twist* who falls into the hands of *Fagin*, whose gang of thieves includes the impudent pickpocket, *the Artful Dodger*, and the villainous *Bill Sikes* with his faithful dog.

A Dickens characters in appropriate settings
SCENES/TITLES
1 Alfred Jingle
2 The Artful Dodger
3 Mrs. Bardell
4 Barkis
5 Barnaby Rudge
6 Bill Sikes (sic)
7 Cap'n Cuttle
8 Mr Chadband
9 Dick Swiveller
10 Mr Dodson
11 Fagin
12 The Fat Boy
13 Little Nell
14 Mark Tapley (two versions)
15 Mr Micawber
16 Old Peggotty
17 Pecksniff
18 Mr Pickwick
19 Poor Jo
20 Sairey Gamp
21 Sam Weller
22 Serjeant Buzfuz
23 Sydney Carton
24 Mr Squeers
25 Tom Pinch
26 Tony Weller
27 Trotty Veck
28 Uriah Heep
29 Mr Toots
30 Newman Noggs
31 Mr Mantalini

Note It is thought that the following characters may also have appeared on Dickensware but so far no examples have come to light:

Betsy Trotwood
Bumble
Daniel Quilp
David Copperfield
Dombey
Dora
Jonas Chuzzlewit
Nancy
The Marchioness
Mrs Nickleby

Dickens. Rack plates, *left to right*, *above* A20, A5, A12, *below* A19, A21, A6

Dickens. Rack plates, *left to right*, *above* A25, A14, A9, *below* A7, A23, A16

Dickens. Rack plates, *left to right*, *above* A24, A15, A22, *below* A14, A18, A26

Dickens. Rack plates, *left to right*, *above* A2, A27, A13, *below* A1, A4, A11

Dickens. Rack plates, *left to right, above* A28, A3, *centre* A10, *below* A17, A8

Poll Sweedlepipe
Snubbin
Mr Winkle

PATTERN NUMBERS
D2973, D3020, D4030, D4069, D5175, D5862, D6327, E8288.

SHAPES
Rack plates, round salad bowl, Corinth teapot, Friar teapot, jug and coffee set, Pelican trinket set, Lennox flower bowl, Rheims cup and saucer, self-pouring teapot, Becket jug, Leeds square and oval fruit dish, chop dish, pin trays, porridge plate, Margot biscuit barrel, hair tidy, hat pin stand, tea caddy, Marcella tobacco jar, Rex mug, Ancestor ashtray, round ashtray, safety match stand, Virginia tobacco jar, candlestick 7277.
Vase numbers 6061, 6886, 7040 A and B, 7012, 7018, 7019, 7265, 7347, 7349, 7350, 7351, 7352, 7353, 7384, 7385, 7391, 7479, 7484, 7538A.

Dickens. Vases, *left to right* A8, A30

DATES

The Dickens series was introduced in 1908 and was augmented in preparation for the centenary of Dickens' birth in February 1912. The range of shapes on which Dickens characters featured was increased in 1917 but by 1930 most had been withdrawn again. In 1931 a more limited series was introduced using a selection of the above characters in a brighter colour scheme. By 1951 production of Dickensware was virtually limited to a few rack plates and a chop dish which made its appearance that year.

Above left: Dickens. *Left to right*, A29, A31

Selection of Dickens ware (catalogue page)

Dickens. *Left to right, above* B2, B3, *below* B6, B5   Dickens. *Above* B1, *below* B4

DESIGNERS
C. J. Noke assisted by William Grace, Walter Nunn, Leonard Langley and Harry Tittensor.

SPECIAL BACKSTAMP

B Groups of Dickens characters

SCENES/TITLES
1 Mr Pickwick with Tupman, Snodgrass and Winkle
2 Pecksniff and his daughters Charity and Mercy
3 The Artful Dodger and Oliver Twist
4 Mr Micawber, his family and David Copperfield
5 Uriah Heep and David Copperfield
6 Little Nell and her grandfather

PATTERN NUMBERS
D2978.

SHAPES
Rack plates, Loving cup 7389.

DATES
In production around 1912.

SPECIAL BACKSTAMP

C Scenes from Dickens

SCENES/TITLES
1 Sairey Gamp
2 The Artful Dodger
3 Tony Weller

PATTERN NUMBERS
No record.

SHAPES
Rack plates, Becket jug.

DATES
In production around 1910.

SPECIAL BACKSTAMP

Dickens. Loving cup B4, jug C1

Dickens. C1, C2, C3

D

SCENES/TITLES
1 Bill Sykes and his dog
2 The Two Wellers

PATTERN NUMBERS
No record.

BORDER
Gold Art Deco.

SHAPES
Rack plates.

DATES
In production around 1930.

E Series modelled in low relief

SCENES/TITLES
1 Fagin
2 The Artful Dodger and Oliver Twist
3 Oliver Twist asks for more
4 Mantolini
5 Mr Pickwick
6 Sam Weller and Mr Pickwick
7 Sam Weller and Mrs Bardell
8 Sam Weller and Tony Weller
9 Tony Weller
10 Tony Weller and Fat Boy
11 Little Nell and grandfather
12 Captain Cuttle and Mr Toots
13 Mr Micawber, Mrs Micawber and David Copperfield
14 Uriah Heep and David Copperfield

Dickens. Rack plates, *left to right* D1, D2

Dickens. Rack plates, *left to right, above* E9, E13, *centre* E11, E12, *below* E1, E2, E7, *bottom* E10, E6

15 Mr Pickwick's Christmas Party
16 David Copperfield and his aunt
Note There may be other characters in this series in various combinations.

PATTERN NUMBERS
D5833.

SHAPES
Rack plates, sandwich tray, oval dish, square teaplate, round shallow bowl, round deep bowl, cream jug, oblong dish, jugs, flagons. These do not feature in the shape guide as they are special shapes for relief decoration.

DATES
This series was introduced in 1937 and . withdrawn during World War II.

F Dickens relief vases
SCENES/TITLES
1 Tony Weller
2 Sam Weller
3 Sairey Gamp
4 Poor Jo and Fat Boy
5 Bill Sykes
6 Nell and grandfather
Note There may be other characters in this series.

PATTERN NUMBERS
D5864.

SHAPES
A variety of specially moulded vases.

DATES
This series was introduced in 1937. The date of withdrawal is not recorded.

Dickens. *Left to right* E5, bowl E3, E4, E8

Dickens. Vases, *left to right* F3, F1, F2, F4

Dickens. Jugs, *left to right* G9, G10, G8, G11, G15

G Dickens relief jugs, flagons and tankards
SCENES/TITLES

1 Old London jug (London in Dickens' day with Old Charley and Sairey Gamp). D6291
2 Peggotty jug (Scene from David Copperfield). D6292
3 Old Curiosity Shop jug (Nell and her grandfather and the Marchioness). D5584
4 Pickwick Papers jug (Mr Pickwick, Sam Weller, Tony Weller and the Fat Boy outside the White Hart Inn). D5756
5 Oliver Twist jug (Oliver, the Artful Dodger, Fagin and Bumble). D5617

6 Oliver Twist jug (Oliver asking for more). D6285
7 Oliver Twist tankard (Oliver and the Artful Dodger). D6286
8 White Hart jug (with Poor Jo and Fat Boy). D5864 and D6394 (two versions)
9 Sairey Gamp jug (with hat handle). D6395
10 Bill Sikes jug. D6396
11 Tony Weller jug. D6397
12 Sam Weller jug. D6398
13 Mask jug with all Dickens' characters and Poor Jo on the handle. (No pattern number recorded)

Dickens. Jugs, *left to right* G4, G1, G2, G7

Dickens. Jugs, *left to right* G5, G3, G6

14 Mask jug depicting Sam Weller, Mr
    Pickwick, Pecksniff, Bill Sikes, Fagin and
    Sydney Carton. D5708
15 Pickwick Papers flagon. (No pattern
    number recorded)

PATTERN NUMBERS
Arranged above for easier identification.

SHAPES
A variety of specially moulded jugs.

DATES
These jugs were introduced in two phases,
1935/7 and 1949–53. They all appear to have
been withdrawn by 1960.

SPECIAL BACKSTAMP

Dickens. Early and late portrait rack plates

H Dickens Portrait

SCENES/TITLES
  1 Bust of Dickens surrounded by sketches of his characters

PATTERN NUMBERS
D2964, D3948, D5900, D6306, TC1042.

COLOURWAYS
Polychrome, sepia and blue and white.

SHAPES
Rack plates.

DATES
The same transfer was issued from 1908 until c1937. On subsequent editions the lettering was slightly altered. The image was redrawn for the translucent china edition in 1968 and this was withdrawn by 1975.

Diversions of Uncle Toby, (Old English Games)

Uncle Toby is taken from Laurence Sterne's (1713–68) novel *Tristam Shandy*. Tristam's uncle, Mr Toby Shandy, is depicted smoking a pipe and wearing black plush breeches. A modest eccentric he spends his time building scale-replicas, complete with trenches, of various military sieges in France. The scenes used by Doulton are a fanciful comment upon the ways in which Uncle Toby may have amused himself.

SCENES/TITLES
  1 'Quoits'
  2 'Skittles'
  3 'The Maypole Dance'
  4 'Cricket'
  5 'Golf'
  6 'Battledore'
  7 'Shuttlecock'
  8 'Quarterstaff'
  9 'Fencing'
  10 'Football'
  11 'As a toxophilite'
  12 Tag
  13 Ale drinking
  14 Tea drinking
  15 'Bowls'

Diversions of Uncle Toby. 3

Diversions of Uncle Toby. *Above* 9, *below* 7, special backstamp

Diversions of Uncle Toby. *Above,* 4, *centre,* 12, *below* 14

SHAPES
Rack plates, jug A, and jug (not in shape guide).

DATES
The series was introduced in 1909 and withdrawn by 1930.

DESIGNER
Walter Nunn.

SPECIAL BACKSTAMP

PATTERN NUMBERS
D3111, D3121, D3197.

COLOURWAYS
Polychrome, Whieldon ware, Holbein glaze.

Diversions of Uncle Toby. Wares, *left to right* 8, 11, 15

Don Quixote

A satirical romance by Miguel de Cervantes (1547–1616), Don Quixote de la Mancha tells the story of a country gentleman who has his wits distorted by heroic tales. Wearing an old suit of armour and mounted on his old horse Rosinante, he sets off on a series of absurd adventures accompanied by his squire, Sancho Panza.

A Scenes from Don Quixote

SCENES/TITLES

1 Don Quixote dreams of performing deeds of valour
2 Burning of the books
3 'The Giants' or 'The fight with the giants'
4 Don Quixote and Sancho Panza knocked senseless
5 Don Quixote being led exhausted to an inn
6 'The Blanket Tossing'
7 'Afterwards'
8 Don Quixote imagines sheep to be an army
9 Don Quixote attacks the sheep
10 Hobbling Rosinante
11 Don Quixote discovers his monster to be a watermill
12 Don Quixote mistakes a barber for a saracen and attacks
13 Don Quixote with the barber's basin believing it to be a golden helmet
14 Don Quixote and the galleyslaves
15 Don Quixote sees the Knight of the Wood
16 Don Quixote defeated by the Knight
17 Don Quixote defeated. 'To do a kindness to a clown is like throwing water in the sea'
18 Don Quixote swears to give up his quest
19 Armorial device: 'Don Quixote de la Mancha'

PATTERN NUMBERS
D2678, D2687, D2690, D2692, D2709, D2970, D2978.

BORDERS
Monsters, fruit and blossom, leaf and berry.

COLOURWAYS
Polychrome, blue and white.

SHAPES
Concord jug, Becket jug, Marcella tobacco jar, Rack plates, Windmill teapot.

DATES
This series was introduced in 1906 and withdrawn in 1928. It is believed there might

have been a later series D4965 introduced in 1929 and withdrawn during World War II but records are not complete on this subject.

B

SCENES/TITLES
1 Don Quixote and Sancho Panza
2 Rear view Don Quixote and Sancho Panza

PATTERN NUMBERS
D3120.

COLOURWAYS
Celadon Ware.

SHAPES
Corinth teapot, rack plates.

DATES
This design was introduced in 1909 and probably also withdrawn around 1928.

C

SCENES/TITLES
1 Portrait of Don Quixote and Sancho Panza

PATTERN NUMBERS
D3683.

BORDER
Trees, sheep and windmill.

SHAPES
Rack plate.

DATES
This design was introduced in 1913 and was withdrawn around 1930.

Don Quixote. *Left and right below* A14, *right above* A1, *right centre* A4

Don Quixote. *Left to right*, *above* A7, A5, *centre* A2, A15. *Below* A9, A10, A8

Don Quixote. A3

Don Quixote. A6

Don Quixote. B2

Gallant Fishers (Izaak Walton)

The Compleat Angler, by Izaak Walton, the first of the English sporting classics was published in 1653 and enjoyed a widespread revival from 1823. This serious discourse on freshwater fishing is enlivened with songs and verse by, among others, Marlowe, Raleigh, Chalkhill and Sir Henry Wotton.

A

SCENES/TITLES
1 'The jealous trout that now did lie
   Rose at a well dissembled fly'
2 'There stood my friend with patient skill
   Attending of his trembling quill'
3 'Of recreation there is none
   So free as fishing is alone'
4 'All other pastimes do no less
   Than mind and body both possess'
5 'My hand alone my work can do
   So I can fish and study too'
6 'And when the timorous trout I wait
   To take, and he devours my bait'
7 'I care not I to fish in seas
   Fresh rivers best my mind do please'
8 'But yet though while I fish I fast
   I make good fortune my repast'
9 'Friend who is more welcome to my dish
   Than to my angle was my fish'
10 'Where in a brook with a hook
   Or a lake fish we take'
11 'None do here, use to swear
   Oaths do fray, fish away'
12 'Perch or Pike, Roach or Dace
   We do chase'
13 'Oh the gallant fishers life it is the best of
   any'
14 'Behold the fisherman, He riseth up early'
Note In many instances two or more of these quotations are used together, for example, the following found on a flowerbowl:
'Oh the gallant fishers life it is the best of any,
And when the timorous trout I wait
To take and he devours my bait'.

CHARACTERS
1 Man with wooden leg
2 Front view of man with one hand in pocket, the other holding the rod vertical
3 Profile man in spectacles grasping a fish
4 Profile man in spectacles with rod under left arm and hand in pocket
5 Profile man in spectacles examining his rod line
6 Profile man in pointed hat with rod over right shoulder and bag in hand

Gallant Fishers. Rack plates with Jedo border, showing characters listed.

7 Profile man with head facing outwards and rod over right shoulder
8 Profile man with large flat hat and rod over left shoulder

Gallant Fishers. Rack plates with willow tree border, showing characters listed.

Below: Selection of Gallant Fishers (Izaak Walton) Ware (catalogue page)

9 Profile man with pointed hat and rod over left shoulder
10 Profile man in short cape and rod over left shoulder
11 Back view with rod over left shoulder
12 Profile man with rod under right arm examining his hook
13 Three-quarter view man with cane and rod over left shoulder

PATTERN NUMBERS
D2312, D2420, D2517, D2704, D3169, D3680, D5959, D5961, E3923.

BORDERS
Japanese, willow tree in green or brown.

SHAPES
Rack plates, Mayfair toilet set, Pelican ashtray, Westcott jug, Loving cup 7058, Virginia tobacco jar.
Jug number 6061.

DATES
A series with no inscriptions and an elaborate Japanese style border known as *Jedo* was introduced in 1901. Later the more common

series with willow tree border and inscriptions was introduced and added to until 1938. It appears to have been discontinued during the Second World War.

DESIGNER
C. J. Noke.

SPECIAL BACKSTAMP

B
SCENES/TITLES
'Izaak Walton, The Compleat Angler.'

PATTERN NUMBERS
D2557.

COLOURWAYS
Whieldon ware.

SHAPES
Tudor jug.

DATES
This design was introduced in 1906. The length of its production is not recorded.

Grimm's Fairy Tales

Joseph and Wilhelm Grimm published a collection of German folk-tales from 1812–15. In *The Six Swans*, the tale illustrated by Doulton, a princess has to remain silent for six years while sewing six shirts in order to turn her six bewitched brothers from swans back to princes.

SCENES/TITLES
1 The princess surrounded by three of the six swans
2 Six flying swans (design for bowl where relevant)

PATTERN NUMBERS
D1544, D1545, D1546, D1564, D2545.

COLOURWAYS
Green and yellow, red and blue, brown and mauve, green and orange.

SHAPES
Rack plates, Mayfair toilet set, Flagon toilet set.

DATES
This design was introduced in 1903. The date of withdrawal is not recorded although it would have been before 1936.

Grimm's Fairy Tales. 1, 2.

Grimm's Fairy Tales. Rack plate, 1

Gulliver's Travels

Written by Jonathan Swift in 1726, *Gulliver's Travels* is a brilliant political satire. Gulliver is shipwrecked on Lilliput where the inhabitants are only six inches tall and the Emperor's pomp and wars are made to look ridiculous. This, and the other adventures that befell Gulliver during his travels were a comment by Swift upon contemporary political and social life.

SCENES/TITLES
1 'I lay in great uneasiness'
2 'The poor man squalled terribly'
3 'The searching of Gulliver featuring 'the snuff box' and 'the watch'
4 'The march under'
5 'Capture of the Fleet'

PATTERN NUMBERS
D2679, D2688, D2691, D2707.

COLOURWAYS
Polychrome, blue and white, sepia.

SHAPES
Becket jug, Marcella tobacco jar.

DATES
The series was introduced in 1906 and withdrawn by about 1928.

Gulliver's Travels. *Left to right, above* 4, 2, 1, *below* 5, 3

Hiawatha

A narrative poem by Henry Longfellow (1807–82), *Hiawatha* is named after an Indian legislator and medicine-man of about 1570. The fictional Hiawatha is the defender and civiliser of his people who lead an idyllic life.

SCENES/TITLES
1 'On his head his eagle feathers. Round his waist his belt of wampum'
2 'Tall of stature. Broad of shoulder. Dark and terrible of aspect'
3 'Crested with great eagle feathers'
4 'Wampum belt and strings and pouches'
5 'Never any deed of daring. But himself has done a bolder'

Hiawatha. Rack plates, *left to right* 5, 1, 2 with 3 different characters and wigwam border

CHARACTERS
Profile Indian, full-face with erect feather headdress, full-face with pig-tails and headdress.

PATTERN NUMBERS
D3044, D5965.

BORDER
Wigwams.

SHAPES
Rack plates, Stein, Regent flower bowl, Loving cup 7058.

DATES
This series was introduced in 1908 and modified in 1938 by adding more colour to the border. It was withdrawn in 1949.

PATTERN NUMBERS
D2532, D6378, E3305.

BORDERS
Ivy wall, rosary beads (bone china version), with selected incidents from the Jackdaw of Rheims story.

SHAPES
Rack plates, Leeds round fruit bowl, Herrick. jug, Scotia jug, Napier ash tray, round salad bowl, chop dish, vase number 7403.

DATES
This series was in production from 1906 until around 1930. A few of the designs were re-introduced in 1949 and feature on isolated items such as the chop dish.

Jackdaw of Rheims

The Jackdaw of Rheims is one of the *Ingoldsby Legends*, a series of verse tales, written by Richard Harris Barham in 1840. It concerns a cheeky Jackdaw who steals the Cardinal's ring but returns it when he suffers from a curse put on the thief. He then becomes so pious he is canonised on his death.

SCENES/TITLES
 1 'The jackdaw sat on the cardinal's chair'
 2 'Bishop and abbot and prior were there'
 3 'Many a monk and many a prior'
 4 'Many a knight and many a squire'
 5 'And they served the Lord Primate on bended knee'
 6 'The Cardinal Lord Archbishop of Rheims'
 7 'And he peered in the face of his Lordships Grace'
 8 'The feast was over the board was cleared'
 9 'Six singing boys dear little souls'
 10 'The Cardinal drew off each plum coloured shoe'
 11 'But no (no such thing) they can't find the ring'
 12 'He called for his candle his bell and his book'
 13 'He solemnly cursed that rascally thief'
 14 'Came limping a poor little lame jackdaw'
 15 'And off that terrible curse he took'
 16 'So they canonized him by the name Jim Crow'
Note On larger items more than one line of the poem is often used.

Jackdaw of Rheims. *Above*, 2, *centre* unrecorded stanza, *below* 9

Jackdaw of Rheims. Fruit bowl 13

Jackdaw of Rheims. *Left to right*, 14, bowl 11, jug 2 with ivy wall border, plate 5 with rosary beads border

Jackdaw of Rheims. *Left to right*, 6, plate 15, jug 10, plate 16

Kismet

Originally a play by Edward Knobloch, published in 1911, Kismet became a musical and then a film. An Arabian Nights fantasy, it features a poet who takes the place of Hajj, a beggar, and becomes involved with the Wazir of police and his wife, Lalume.

SCENES/TITLES

1 Hajj Hajj
2 Hajj in the Bazaar
3 Hajj before Mansur
4 The Caliph
5 Marsinah, Hajj and Nargis
6 Caliph and Marsinah
7 Marsinah and Nargis

Kismet scenes

PATTERN NUMBERS
No record.

SHAPES
No record.

DATES
The transfers appear in the pattern book dated c1905.

Omar Khayyam

The Rubaiyat of Omar Khayyam (c1100), astronomer and poet, is a series of stanzas meditating on the mysteries of existence. Fitzgerald, in his translations of 1859, gave them a connected train of thought and emphasised the pleasure-loving aspects.

SCENES/TITLES
'*Omar Khayyam*
The moving finger writes and having writ
Moves on, nor all the Piety nor Wit
Shall lure it back to cancel half a line
Nor all thy tears wash out a word of it'.

PATTERN NUMBERS
D3287, D3288, D3289.

COLOURWAYS
Blue and white, Holbein glaze, Whieldon ware.

SHAPES
Rack plates.

DATES
This design was in production from 1910 until 1928.

Rip Van Winkle

Washington Irving's Americanised version of a European folk-tale, *Rip Van Winkle* (1819) tells the tale of a man who goes into the mountains, drinks a magic potion tasting of Hollands Gin, and wakes up twenty years later. Arthur Rackham produced an illustrated version in 1904 which inspired the second Doulton series.

A
SCENES/TITLES
1 'Surrounded by a troop of children. Taught them fly kites'.

Omar Khayyam. Rack plate

2 Rip with one of the 'odd looking persons' on his shoulders.
3 'Their visages too were peculiar'.
4 'Much the flavour of excellent Hollands'.
5 'Answered by a flock of idle crows'.
6 'My very dog has forgotten me'.
Note On many items more than one of the above scenes are featured.

PATTERN NUMBERS
D2553, D2554, D2555.

BORDERS
Plain, or grapevine.

COLOURWAYS
Polychrome, blue and white, Whieldon ware.

SHAPES
Rack plates, Tavern jug, Concord jug.

DATES
This series was introduced in 1906 and was probably eventually replaced by Series B.

DESIGNER
Walter Nunn

B
SCENES/TITLES
1 'They clambered up a narrow gully'.
2 'A company of odd looking persons playing at nine pins'.
3 'Those fairy mountains'.
4 'The draught of Hollands'.
5 'The sleep of Rip van Winkle'.

Rip Van Winkle. *Above* A1, A2, *below* A6, A5

Rip Van Winkle. *Left to right* A4, A3

Rip Van Winkle. *Left to right* B3 & B4, B2, B5 & B3, A2

6 'Eying him from head to foot with great curiosity'.

7 'When I last saw him he was a venerable old man'.

Note On many items more than one of the above scenes are featured.

PATTERN NUMBERS
D2788, D2894.

BORDERS
Oak leaf.

SHAPES
Rack plates, Teapot B, Hecla jug.

DATES
This series was introduced in 1907 and was in production until about 1928.

Shakespeare

William Shakespeare (1564–1616) is one of the world's most familiar playwrights. His universal popularity encouraged C. J. Noke to design many Series wares for Doulton illustrating characters, scenes and quotations from his plays, and places and people associated with his life and family.

The following plays and characters are featured:
As You Like It: Rosalind, Touchstone, Audrey, Orlando, Ganymede, Celia
Cymbeline: Imogen, Iachimo
Hamlet: Hamlet, Ophelia
Henry IV: Falstaff, Prince Henry
Henry VIII: Katherine, Wolsey, Henry VIII
King Lear: Goneril, Regan, Cordelia, Lear
Macbeth: Lady Macbeth
Merchant of Venice: Portia, Shylock, Bassanio
Merry Wives of Windsor: Fenton, Falstaff, Anne Page, Dame Quickly

Shakespeare. *Left to right, above* A9, A11, *below* A10, A6

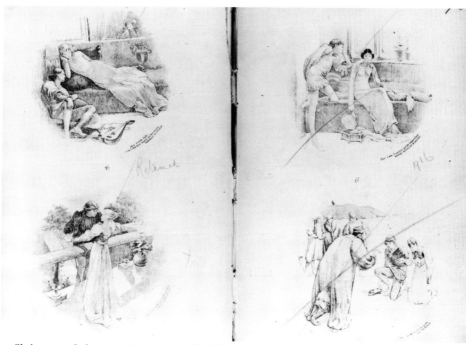

Shakespeare. *Left to right, above* A3, A4, *below* A8, A5

Shakespeare. A2

Midsummer Night's Dream: Titania, Tom Snout, Snug, Bottom
Much Ado About Nothing: Beatrice, The Watch
Othello: Desdemona, Othello
Pericles: Pericles, Marina
Romeo and Juliet: Romeo, Juliet, Friar Lawrence
Tempest: Miranda, Gonzales
Twelfth Night: Sir Toby Belch, Sir Andrew Aguecheek
Winter's Tale: Autolycus

Shakespeare. *Above* A12, *below* A7

A

SCENES/TITLES

1 *'Winter's Tale* Aut: Lawn as white as driven snow'
2 *'Much Ado About Nothing* Beat: Against my will, I am sent to bid you come to dinner'
3 *'Merchant of Venice* Bass.: Gentle Lady, When did I first impart my love to you'
4 *'Merry Wives of Windsor* Fent.: I see I cannot get thy father's love'
5 *'The Tempest* Gon.: Look down ye gods'
6 *'The Tempest* Mira.: Sweet Lord, you play me false'
7 *'Romeo and Juliet* Rom.: To smooth that rough touch with a tender kiss' *and*
8 *'Romeo and Juliet* Rom.: Farewell, farewell one kiss'
9 *'As You Like It* It was a lover and his lass'
10 *'As You Like It* Ros.: Do you hear, forester?'
11 *'As You Like It* Touch.: It is meat and drink to me to see a clown'
12 *'As You Like It* Under the Greenwood Tree'

PATTERN NUMBERS
D357, D914, D2137, D2543. Most do not have a D mark.

BORDERS
Lacy with flowers and scrolls, garland scrolls and basket, urn swags and flowers.

COLOURWAYS
Sepia, blue and white.

SHAPES
Stafford dessert plate, Egerton plate, Ornate teapot (not in shape guide).

DATES
These designs were mentioned in the Pottery Gazette, August 1899. The range of shapes on which they were used increased until 1906 when they were superseded in popularity by other Shakespearean series. There is no record of the final withdrawal date.

Shakespeare. Rack plates, *above* A1 with garland scrolls and basket border, *centre* A11 with urn, swags and flowers border, *below* A9 with lacy flowers and scroll border

Shakespeare. *Left to right, above* B2, B1, *below* B9, B10

B Shakespeare's Plays

SCENES/TITLES

1 '*Midsummer Night's Dream* Act IV Scene 1. The Wood. Come sit thee down upon this flowery bank. While I thy amiable cheeks do coy' (Titania and Bottom)

2 *Romeo and Juliet* Act III Scene 5. (Romeo and Juliet)

3 *Romeo and Juliet* Act III Scene 3 (or Act II Scene 3). (Romeo and Friar Lawrence)

4 *Merchant of Venice* Act IV Scene 1. (Shylock and Portia)

5 *Macbeth* Act V Scene 1. (Lady Macbeth sleepwalking)

6 *As You Like It* Act II Scene 4. (Touchstone with Ganymede (Rosalind) and Celia)

7 *Merry Wives of Windsor* Act III Scene 1. (Falstaff in a basket)

8 *Henry VIII* Act I Scene 2. (Henry and Wolsey)

9 *Pericles, Prince of Tyre* Act V Scene 1. (Pericles and Marina)

10 *Lear* Act I Scene 1. (Lear and his three daughters)

11 *Cymbeline* Act II Scene 2. (Iachimo and Imogen)

12 *Othello* Act V Scene 2 (Othello and Desdemona)

PATTERN NUMBERS
D1771, D1772, D1773, D2129, D3199, D3666, D4392.

BORDERS
Stylised acanthus, pink stencil, simple garland, small flowers, stylised flower and fluted, black band.

COLOURWAYS
Polychrome, blue and white.

SHAPES
Rack plates, spittoon, Regent flower bowl, pedestal (not in shape guide).

DATES
This series was introduced in 1903, with new border designs and colourways being added until the end of the First World War. It had been completely withdrawn by 1928.

DESIGNER
H. Watson.

Shakespeare. *Left to right*, *above* B7, B5, *below* B4, B6

Shakespeare. *Left to right*, *above* B12, B8, *below* B3, B11

Shakespeare. Rack plate, B1 with stylised acanthus border

Shakespeare. Rack plate, B8 with small flower border

C Falstaff

SCENES/TITLES

1 '*Merry Wives of Windsor* Act II Scene 2. Falstaff and Dame Quickly: I warrant thee nobody hears'.
2 '*Henry IVth Part I* Act III Scene 3. Falstaff: Do thou amend thy face. And I'll amend my life. Thou art our admiral. Thou bearest the lantern in the poop—but 'tis the nose of thee, Thou art the knight of the burning lamp'.
3 '*Henry IVth Part II* Act II Scene 4. Prince Henry: Why thou Globe of Sinful Continents, What a life thou dost lead'.

PATTERN NUMBERS
D2779, D2826, D2881.

BORDERS
Checkered.

SHAPES
Rack plates, Flagon toilet set, Premier jug.

DATES
This series was introduced in 1907 and withdrawn by 1928.

SPECIAL BACKSTAMP

D Shakespearean Knights

SCENES/TITLES

1 Sir Toby Belch, occasionally with the quotation 'Maria, I say a stoop of wine'
2 Sir Andrew Aguecheek
3 Sir John Falstaff

PATTERN NUMBERS
D1978, D2220, D2373, D2493, D2494, D2495, D4750.

COLOURWAYS
Polychrome, sepia.

SHAPES
Rack plates, spittoon, Stein, Lennox flower bowl, Baron jug.

DATES
This series was introduced in 1904 with variations in shapes and colourways introduced over the next two years. It was withdrawn by 1928.

DESIGNER
C. J. Noke.

47

Shakespeare. Rack plates, *left to right*, *above* C2, C1, *centre* C3, below E1, E2

Shakespeare. E3

E Dogberry's Watch

SCENES/TITLES

1 Watchman with pike and lantern. '1st
Watch: This man sir said that Don John

the Prince's Brother was a villain'.
2 Bearded man with cane pointing. 'Sexton,
what heard you him say else?'
3 Grumpy man with hand on keys (quotation
not recorded).
Note Two different backgrounds are known
consisting of either a row of half-timbered
houses or a procession of other watchmen.

PATTERN NUMBERS
D2644, D2699, D2721, D2722.

SHAPES
Rack plates, Stroon jug, Regent flower bowl,
Marcella tobacco jar.

DATES
This series was introduced in 1906 and
withdrawn by 1928.

DESIGNER
C. J. Noke.

Shakespeare. Rack plates, *left to right* D3, D1, D2

Shakespeare. F4

F Midsummer Night's Dream

CHARACTERS
1 Snout
2 Snug
3 Bottom
4 Titania

PATTERN NUMBERS
D2874.

SHAPES
Faceted rack plates (not in shape guide),
Teapot B, Hecla jug and Hecla salad bowl.

DATES
This series was introduced in 1907 and
withdrawn by 1928.

SPECIAL BACKSTAMP

Shakespeare. *Left to right*, F1, F2, F3

Shakespeare. Rack plates. *Left to right, above* G4, G6, G12, *below* G1, G3, G5

Shakespeare. Rack plates. *Left to right, above* G9, G8, G10, *below* G11, G7, G2

G Shakespearean Characters in appropriate settings

CHARACTERS
1 Romeo
2 Juliet
3 Shylock
4 Portia
5 Hamlet
6 Ophelia
7 Anne Page
8 Falstaff
9 Katharine
0 Wolsey
1 Orlando
2 Rosalind

PATTERN NUMBERS
D3596, D3746, D3835, D3882, D4070, E7267.

COLOURWAYS
Sepia background (with polychrome figure), or entirely polychrome.

SHAPES
Rack plates, Stafford dessert plate, Leeds round fruit dish, celery tray, sandwich tray, porridge plate, round fruit saucer, Pelican trinket set, Canute cheese stand, Joan tea service, Rheims teacup and saucer, Durham fern pot, hair tidy, hat pin stand, Lennox flower bowl, Corinth jugs, Rocket jug, Rex mug, round salad bowl, tea caddy, safety match stand, Mayfair toilet set, candlestick 277.
Vase numbers 6061, 7040A, 7347, 7348, 7382, 7383, 7386, 7397, 7410.

DATES
This series was introduced in 1912 with a polychrome background. In 1914 the range of shapes was augmented and a new sepia background was introduced. Additions with slight background modifications were made to the range until the First World War and it appears to have been finally withdrawn by 1928.

H Midsummer Night's Dream

SCENES/TITLES
'The Blessing Ceremony'

PATTERN NUMBERS
None recorded.

DATES
1922.

Shakespearian Series $\frac{D}{5}$ 3746.

Selection of Shakespeare wares (catalogue page)

Shakespeare. H1

Shakespeare's country. Rack plates, *left to right, above* I5, I4, I3, *below* I2, I1

Shakespeare. Rack plates, *above* birthday commemorative, *below* J2 (two versions)

Shakespeare's Country
SCENES/TITLES
1 Papist Wixford
2 Beggarly Broom
3 Anne Hathaway's Cottage
4 Aston Cantlow
5 Guy's Cliff House
6 Guy's Cliff Mill
7 Charlecote
8 Bidford
9 Kenilworth Castle

PATTERN NUMBERS
D4149, V2354.

SHAPES
Rack plates, Tavern jug, Joan tea service, Stafford dessert plate, Leeds oval, round and square fruit dish, porridge plate, Regent tea service, Lennox flower bowl, round salad bowl, sandwich tray, celery tray, Rheims cup and saucer, Marcella tobacco jar.
Vase numbers 7349, 7385, 7386.

DATES
This series was introduced in 1921 and withdrawn by 1939. The subjects illustrated on this series either have connections with Shakespeare and his family, or depict local scenes around Stratford.

J Shakespeare's Portrait
SCENES/TITLES
1 Bust of Shakespeare
2 Bust of Shakespeare surrounded by sketches of his characters (two versions)

PATTERN NUMBERS
D3194, D3195, D3253, D5910, D6302, D6303, TC1041.

COLOURWAYS
Polychrome, blue and white, sepia, black.

SHAPES
1 recorded on Westcott jug with oak leaf border
2 on rack plates, Egerton plates, Westcott jug

DATES
The design was first used in 1909 in various colourways. It was redrawn with very slight modifications in 1938 and again in 1948, remaining in production until 1967 when it was replaced by the translucent china version which used the same imagery but drawn in a different style. The china version was

withdrawn in 1975. There was also a commemorative rack plate sponsored by the 1964 Shakespeare Anniversary Council, Stratford-Upon-Avon, depicting Shakespeare and inscribed 'To commemorate the 400th Anniversary of the Birth of William Shakespeare'.

Sir Roger de Coverley
One of a number of fanciful characters created by Thomas Steele for *The Spectator*, a literary magazine first published in 1711–12, Sir Roger is depicted as the perfect country gentleman. He is shown at work and play, in love, as a good churchman and strong Tory. His neighbours include Tom Touchy, who sues everyone he can, and a landlord who models his sign on Sir Roger's head.

SCENES/TITLES
1 Mr Spectator reading an invitation to be a guest of Sir Roger
2 Sir Roger and Mr Spectator playing bowls.
3 Dining on the fish presented by Mr Wimble. 'How the Jack was caught'
4 Sir Roger besotted by the widow in a garden
5 Sir Roger visiting the widow in her parlour
6 Sir Roger dancing with the widow
7 'Sir Roger's ancestor invents a new mode of making love'

Sir Roger de Coverley. *Above* 9, *below left* 17, *right* 12

Sir Roger de Coverley. *Left, above* 10, *below* 11, *right* 16

Sir Roger de Coverley. *Left, above* 1, *centre* 4, *below* 5, *right* 2

Sir Roger de Coverley. *Left to right, above* 6, 15, *centre* 17, 7, 13, *below* 2, 8, 1, 10

8 Mr William with a young maid in the garden
9 Sir Roger with children in church
10 Sir Roger with one of his servants 'Happy if they could open a gate'
11 Sir Roger's groom. 'The grey pad'
12 'Tom Touchy'
13 Tom Touchy receiving visitors in his library
14 Sir Roger as a magistrate in court
15 Sir Roger in *The Saracen's Head* looking at the altered sign
16 Sir Roger travelling to London
17 The Spectators return to town

PATTERN NUMBERS
D3418, D5000, D5814.

BORDERS
Plain, or tree and bird border.

SHAPES
Rack plates, Westcott jug, Corinth tea service, round salad bowl, Marcella tobacco jar. Vase number 7023.

DATES
This series was introduced in 1911. Changes were made to the range in 1930 and 1937 and it was withdrawn by 1949.

SPECIAL BACKSTAMP

Treasure Island

A boys' romance by Scotsman Robert Louis Stevenson (1850–94), *Treasure Island* is as popular today as when it was written. The arrival of Blind Pew at the Admiral Benbow Inn leads to the discovery of a map of Captain Kidd's treasure. Young Jim Hawkins, Squire Trelawney and Captain Smollett set sail in the *Hispaniola* to find it, unaware that the crew, led by Long John Silver, are pirates.

SCENES/TITLES
1 Long John Silver with treasure map, sailors unloading supplies behind
2 Long John Silver with parrot in hand
3 Long John Silver holding parrot with wings outstretched
4 Long John Silver directing sailor with pickaxe
5 Long John Silver seated, waving crutch
6 Long John Silver with Jim Hawkins (two versions)
7 Captain Smollett
8 The Boy Jim
9 Jim Hawkins and sailor spying through telescope
10 Sailor climbing rigging
11 Sailors in a rowing boat
12 Blind Pew
Note Also incidental groups featuring the treasure chest, views of the island, barrels, ropes and anchors.

PATTERN NUMBERS
D5812, D6376.

Treasure Island. *Left* 1, *right*, *above* 5, 12, *centre* 10, *below* 9, 7

Treasure Island. *Left to right*, *above* 4, 2, *below* 3

Treasure Island. *Left* 8, *right* 7, 11, and incidental groups

Treasure Island. Chop dish, 1

SHAPES
Rack plates, chop dish, Quorn jug.

DATES
The series was first recorded in 1934 but appears to have been marketed from 1937 onwards. Modifications were made to the range in 1950. The date of withdrawal is not known although it would have been before 1967.

Uncle Tom's Cabin

This famous anti-slavery novel by Harriet Beecher Stowe (1811–96) features the old black slave, Uncle Tom and Haley the evil slave trader.

SCENES/TITLES
1 'Haley packs up Uncle Tom for the down south market'
2 'Scenes daily and hourly acting under the shadow of American law'
3 'The human commodities under inspection'
4 'The article suggests another proprietor of sails'
5 'Death of Little Eva, the last of earth'
6 'Death of Uncle Tom'

PATTERN NUMBERS
No record.

SHAPES
No record.

DATES
The transfers appear in the pattern book dated c1905.

Uncle Tom's Cabin. *Left to right, above* 1, 2, 3, *below* 4, 5, 6

Under the Greenwood Tree (Robin Hood)

The legendary hero of Sherwood Forest in Nottinghamshire, whose followers included the jovial Friar Tuck, giant Little John and Alan a Dale, Robin Hood stole from the rich to give to the poor. He rescued Maid Marion from Guy of Gisborne whom he later slew. The outlaws were pardoned by King Richard I when he eventually returned from the Crusades.

SCENES/TITLES

1 'Robin Hood, the friend of the poor' (two versions
2 'Robin Hood's fight with Friar Tuck'
3 'Friar Tuck joins Robin Hood' or 'The jovial friar joins Robin Hood' (the Friar's staff is at a different angle in the latter)
4 'Robin Hood and Friar Tuck'
5 'Robin Hood and Little John'
6 'Alan a Dale'
7 'Robin Hood'
8 'Maid Marion'
9 'Robin Hood and Maid Marion'
10 'Robin Hood, the King of the Archers' (two versions, one of which includes Alan a Dale)

Under the Greenwood Tree. 17

11 'The Foresters Kitchen'
12 'Friar Tuck makes merry under the greenwood tree' or 'Under the greenwood tree'
13 'Robin Hood, Little John and Jovial Friar Tuck'
14 'Robin Hood in ambush'
15 'Robin Hood kneels to the King'
16 'Robin Hood slays Guy of Gisborne'
17 'Life in the Forest of Sherwood'

Under the Greenwood Tree. Rack plates, *above* 14, *centre* 15, *below* 16, *bottom* 1

Under the Greenwood Tree. Selection of wares, *left to right* 9, 12, 4, 13

Under the Greenwood Tree. Selection of wares, *left to right*, *above* 3, 17, *below* 6, 2, 10, 10 (2nd version)

PATTERN NUMBERS
D3751, D5808, D6094, D6341.

SHAPES
Rack plates, Lennox flower bowl, Regent fern pot, Leeds round fruit dish, ice jug, Newlyn jugs, baby plate, Pelican trinket set, tea caddy, Marcella tobacco jar, Clive tea service, stein, celery tray, porridge plate, oatmeal saucer, fruit saucer, round salad bowl, Rex mug, Rheims teacup and saucer, Ancestor ashtray, cruet set (not in shape guide), candlestick 7277, Loving cups numbers 7348, 7389, Mayfair toilet set, sandwich tray, beaker, teapot.
Vase numbers 7013, 7014, 7015, 7016, 7017, 7018, 7019, 7023, 7040A and B, 7350, 7383, 7384, 7385, 7386, 7387, 7388, 7397, 7429, 7444, 7465.

DATES
This series was introduced in 1914, with slight modifications and additional items appearing in 1937, 1939 and 1951. It was finally withdrawn in 1967.

SPECIAL BACKSTAMP

58

Willow Pattern Story

This familiar chinoiserie tableware pattern was first developed in Staffordshire during the 1780s. Its immediate popularity made it a standard blue-printed design for most tableware manufacturers during the 19th century. Although the motifs in the design were broadly Chinese in style, the whole conception was totally European. The legend associated with the design, and here developed by Doulton, was invented by some unknown artist probably early in the 19th century.

A

SCENES/TITLES
1 Koongshee and Chang escape over the bridge. 'Chang and Koongshee escape but are pursued by the Tipsy Mandarin whom they elude'.
2 Escape from the gardener's cottage by boat. 'After living in the gardener's cottage where they had taken refuge from pursuit, they escape in a boat to avoid arrest by the soldiers'.
3 They arrive at an island. 'After travelling many miles they moor their boat beside an island covered with reeds and there resolve to settle down and spend their days in peace'.
4 Chang cultivates the island. 'They purchased a free right to the little island and having built a house, and from the sale of jewels, obtained all that was necessary. Chang brought the island into a high state of cultivation'.
5 Chang and Koongshee on the island. 'Here they lived happily'.
6 Chang writes a book. 'Chang having achieved a competence by his cultivation of the land, returned to his literary pursuits and wrote a book on agriculture which gained for him great reputation'

PATTERN NUMBERS
D4478, D4851, E7211, E7831, E7832.

Willow Pattern Story. Rack plates, *Above* A1, A2 *Below* A4, A5 with bird and swirl border

BORDERS
Bird and swirl, Japanese with medallions containing other incidents in the story, blue roses.

COLOURWAYS
Polychrome, sepia, blue and white, mauve and black.

SHAPES
Rack plates, octagon plate, Cecil teacup and saucer.

DATES
This series was introduced around 1920 and withdrawn by 1945.

B Motoring Willow Pattern

SCENES/TITLES
A humorous interpretation of the Willow Pattern conventions depicting motoring exploits.

PATTERN NUMBERS
D3625.

SHAPES
Rack plates.

DATES
This design was introduced in 1912 but the date of withdrawal is not recorded although it would have been before 1936.

Motoring Willow pattern

Willow Pattern Story.
Rack plates, *above* A3, *below* A6

Zodiac

The sun's path around Earth is divided,
astrologically, into twelve sections, each
associated with particular characteristics of
human behaviour: Aries, thrusting and
pioneering; Taurus, stolid and calm; Gemini,
showing dichotomy; Cancer, mother-love; Leo,
leadership and success; Virgo, mutable and
earthy; Libra, gentle and affectionate; Scorpio,
great strength; Sagittarius, joviality;
Capricorn, organised and disciplined;
Aquarius, innovative; Pisces, a dreamer.

SCENES/TITLES
1 The globe surrounded by zodiac symbols.

PATTERN NUMBERS
D3112.

COLOURWAYS
Whieldon ware, blue and white.

SHAPES
Rack plates.

DATES
This design was introduced in 1909. The date
of withdrawal is not recorded, although it
would have been before 1936.

Zodiac

Aldin's Dogs. A3 (advertising leaflet)

Aldin. Old English Scenes (catalogue page)

Aldin. Selection of wares, *left to right*, plate B2, teapot B7, plate B3, sweet dish A2, jug A4, A5

Popular Illustrators

Aldin

Cecil Aldin (1870–1935) popular book illustrator and master of the travel poster is best known for his ubiquitous mongrel dog, alternately impudent or woeful which featured in many of his books, in particular *A Dog's Day*, *Dogs of Character* and his autobiography *Time I was Dead*. These humorous studies were featured on a wide range of series ware as were his acclaimed hunting and country scenes.

A Aldin's Dogs
CHARACTERS
1 Dog staring at trophy
2 Dog with rope
3 Dog smoking pipe
4 Smiling dog's head with ears sticking out
5 Three-quarter view dog's head with tongue out
6 Front view dog's head

PATTERN NUMBERS
D4525, D4629.

BORDERS
Plain or acanthus.

COLOURWAYS
Polychrome, Titanian glaze.

SHAPES
Rack plates, Cleveland teapot, Corinth tea service, Octagon sweet dish

DATES
This series was introduced in 1926 and withdrawn by 1946.

B Old English Scenes
SCENES/TITLES
1 Mounted huntsman with dogs
2 Mounted huntsman looking down at dogs
3 Horse and cart being led to the inn
4 Horse and cart being led away from the inn
5 The inn
6 Two country folk outside the inn
7 Horse and cart being led to a village where a woman is feeding chickens

PATTERN NUMBERS
D4507, D4723.

SHAPES
Rack plates, Westcott jug, Windmill teapot, Harlech teacup and saucer, Leeds square fruit dish, round salad bowl, Napier ashtray, Vase numbers 7040A, 7397.

DATES
This series was introduced in 1926. The date of withdrawal is not recorded.

Bateman

Henry Mayo Bateman (1887–1970) the popular social satirist contributed humorous drawings to most of the leading magazines of the 'twenties and 'thirties, in particular *Punch* and *The Tatler*. He is best remembered for his 'The Man who' drawings where some unfortunate individual inadvertently makes some terrible *faux pas*. His gift for caricature

Bateman. *Left to right, above* 12, 11, 13, 14, *centre* 10, 8, 7, *below* 9

Bateman. *Left to right* Stein 5, 6, box 4, pin tray 1

Bateman selection (advertising photograph)

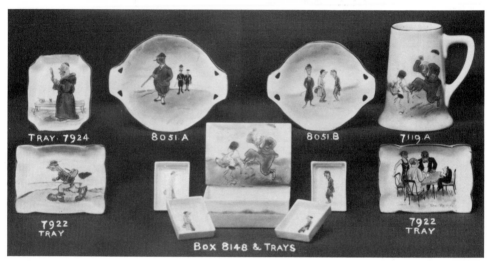

TRAY. 7924   8051.A   8051.B   7119.A

7922 TRAY

BOX 8148 & TRAYS

7922 TRAY

can be seen at its best in what he called his 'types' based on acute observation which predominate in the Doulton series.

CHARACTERS
1 The monk
2 The fisherman
3 The game hunter
4 The irate golfer
5 The smug golfer with club behind his back
6 The laughing caddies
7 Boxers preparing
8 The punch
9 The knockout
10 The card game
11 The officer
12 The officer with monocle
13 Soldiers marching
14 Soldier presenting arms

PATTERN NUMBER
D5813.

SHAPES
Octagon sweet dish, Stein, playing card box, cigarette box, pin trays (not in shape guide).

DATES
This series was first recorded in 1930 but does not appear to have been marketed until 1937. It was withdrawn around 1950.

Bradley

Will H. Bradley (1868–1930) was one of the pioneers of the artistic poster in America, his best known commissions being for the *Chap Book* and the *Century* magazines. His style is closely derived from Beardsley, employing the same serpentine line and embroidered detail but without the sinister connotations of the master's work. Many of the designs adapted by Doulton are from *Bradley, His*

3radley. *Left to right, above* A1, A2, A3, A5, *below* A3, A4, A7, A13

Bradley. *Left to right, above* A9, A7, A10, A12, *below* A15, A8, A14, A6, A4, A11, *sideways* A7

Bradley. Jardiniere showing characters A10, A12 and grapevine border

Book Vol 1 No 4, 1896 which featured his illustrations for *Beauty and the Beast*.

A Eastern Figures

CHARACTERS

1 Bearded Eastern character with arms folded
2 Couple with lady enveloped in man's cloak
3 Gentleman resting on a cane wearing extremely pointed shoes

4 Lady carrying a tray of fruit
5 Lady in profile with full gown making a sinuous silhouette
6 Front view of above lady
7 Lady in long fringed gown and shorter cloak carrying a cane
8 Couple arm in arm on a bench
9 Gentleman with ornate sword hilt under his cloak

Bradley. *Left to right, above* B4, B13, B14, B9, *centre* B8, B6, B2, B11, B7, B1, *below* B5, B3, B12, B16, A10, B3, B2, A9, B10, *bottom* A6, A3, B15, B5, B8

Bradley. *Left to right above* B19, B18, *below* B17

10 Gentleman with a lute
11 Lady in short dress dancing with a fan
12 Lady holding the skirts of her short dress in both hands
13 Lady in short style flared skirt
14 Gentleman in profile leaning on a cane
15 Gentleman with arms outstretched holding a cane
Note These figures either appear singly or in various combinations against several backgrounds including rose and trellis, stylised art nouveau trees, gilt flowers on a black ground.

PATTERN NUMBERS
D540, D943, D947, D1017, D1020, D1027, D1036, D1126, D1127, D1242, D1263, D1386, D1432, D1475, D2043, D2044, D2051, D2061, D2117, D2227.

BORDERS
Grapevine, stylised leaves or Renaissance style swags and cartouches used with top half of the above figures.

COLOURWAYS
Blue and white with gold, green and blue, brown, green and gold.
Whieldon ware, Holbein glaze (Morrisian ware).

SHAPES
Breda jug, Ball teapot, Regent flower bowl, Tudor jug, Marcella tobacco jar, Castle jug. Vase number 6730 Jug B.
Also many early shapes not included in the shape guide.

DATES
These designs were introduced in 1901 with new shapes and colourways continually being added to the series until 1905. The exact date of withdrawal is not known although it was probably during World War I.

B Golfers
CHARACTERS
1 Back view lady golfer
2 Front view lady golfer
3 Profile lady golfer
4 Golfer poised to putt, three-quarter view
5 Golfer poised to putt, profile
6 Golfer poised to putt, front view
7 Profile golfer in energetic swing
8 Bare-headed golfer in swing before hit
9 Front view golfer in swing before hit
10 Front view golfer in swing before hit (with boots)
11 Front view golfer in swing after hit
12 Front view golfer in swing after hit (buckle shoes)

Bradley. Rack plates, *left to right, above* C5, C2, C7, *below* C4, C1, C6, with grapevine border on C6, C7, the remainder with stylised floral border

13 Profile golfer in swing before hit
14 Profile golfer in swing after hit
15 Profile golfer in swing after hit (with cloak)
16 Back view golfer in energetic swing
17 Caddy with clubs on his back
18 Caddy leaning on the golf bag
19 Caddy taking a club from the bag
Note The golfers either appear singly or in various combinations against several backgrounds including stylised art nouveau trees, gilt flowers, and trees on a dark ground. Occasionally golfers and Eastern figures appear together on the same items.

PATTERN NUMBERS
D1132, D1165, D1385, D1395, D1396, D1398, D1424, D1430, D1464, D2227.

BORDERS
Grapevine, floral with historic views set in cartouches.

COLOURWAYS
Blue and white, green and yellow, Whieldon ware, Holbein glaze.

SHAPES
Rack plates, Ceylon teapot, Breda jug, Ball teapot, Kendal teapot, Lennox flower bowl, Baron jug, Tudor jug.

DATES
These designs first appeared in 1902 with new shapes and colourways being added to the series until 1905. The exact date of withdrawal is not known although it was probably during World War I.

C Proverbs
SCENES/TITLES
1 'If at first you don't succeed try again
   A miss is as good as a mile'
2 'Fine Feathers Make Fine Birds
   Old Saws speak the truth'

3 'Hope springs eternal in the human breast
  Hope deferred maketh the heart sink'
4 'An oak is not felled by one blow
  Take the will for the deed'
5 'Nothing venture nothing win
  Count not your chickens before they are
  hatched'
6 'Fine feathers make fine birds
  Handsome is that handsome does'
7 'Nothing venture nothing have
  A bird in the hand is worth two in the bush'
Note Proverbs were used in conjunction with
several Bradley style figures.

PATTERN NUMBERS
D3391, D3481.

BORDERS
Grapevine, stylised floral.

SHAPES
Rack plates.

DATES
These designs were introduced in 1911 and
withdrawn by 1928.

Caldecott

Randolph Caldecott (1846–86), despite
receiving only a slight training in art, is one of
the most popular humorous illustrators of all
time. He is remembered both for his book
illustrations, for example for Washington Irving's
Old Christmas and the children's series which
includes *The House That Jack Built* and for his
cartoons for magazines such as *Punch*.
Featured by Doulton are drawings for the *New
York Daily Graphic* which were reproduced in
book form: Our Haymaking and Mr Carlyon's
Christmas from *Graphic*; Christmas Visitors
(1876) from *Gleanings from the Graphic*; The
Curmudgeons' Christmas and A Hunting
Family from *Last Graphic Pictures*.

Christmas Visitors from my Grandfather's Sketches
SCENES/TITLES
1 'The old folks'
2 'The young folks'
3 'The Christmas wine'
4 The young Squire entertains some
  hunting friends
5 'The coachman mixes a Christmas bowl'

Caldecott. Rack plates, *above* 1, *below* 2, leaf and
berry border

Mr. Carlyon's Christmas as noted in his
diary pictured by his grandson RC.
6 *23rd Dec*. Delayed by deep snows on road to
  Shropshire
7 Stopped by two highwaymen
8 Overthrew the highwaymen and captured
  them
9 *2nd Jan*. Snow gone so hunting party
  formed. Found a fox in laurels. I took
  the lead and gave it to Diana
10 I had to admonish Squire Mallow for
  riding dangerously
11 Pleasant ride home with Diana

Caldecott. *Above* 5, *below* 13

Caldecott. *Above* 3, 14, *centre* 9, *below* 9, 10, 11

Caldecott. *Above* 6, *centre* 7, *below* 8

Caldecott. *Upper page* 12, 4, *lower page* 19, 18, 20

The Curmudgeon's Christmas
12 Host spooning punch
13 Disagreement at breakfast
14 The toast

Our Haymaking
15 The Mowing
16 The Tedding
17 The Carrying

A Hunting Family
18 The arrival of the Huntbatches at the cover-side and anxiety of the Master of the Hounds
19 Fox gone away—burning scent—Huntbatch family in full cry
20 Return of the Huntbatches to Oak Hall

PATTERN NUMBERS
D2969.

BORDERS
Leaf and berry

SHAPES
Rack plates, round salad bowl, Windmill teapot, Regent flower bowl, spittoon, Premier jug, Clent jug.

DATES
The series was introduced in 1908. The date of withdrawal is not recorded although it would have been before 1936.

Caldecott. *Above* 16, *centre* 15, *below* 17

Gibson

Charles Dana Gibson (1867–1944) was a brilliant American illustrator whose satires appeared frequently in magazines such as *Life*, *The Century* and *Harpers Weekly*. Through his most popular creation, 'The Gibson Girl', he wittily commented on the social life of his times. This Edwardian beauty rapidly became a cult figure, exploited by the commercial world and appearing on objects as diverse as fans and wall papers. The Doulton series ware illustrations are taken from Gibson's books *Drawings* 1898, *Americans* 1900, *A Widow and her Friends* 1901, *The Social Ladder* 1902.

A
CHARACTERS
1 Gibson Girl heads: 12 different poses

BORDERS
Blue and white lovers' knots and hearts.

COLOURWAYS
Sepia or black.

SHAPES
Rack plates only.

DATES
These designs were introduced in 1901 although many of the designs appear on old stock plates with earlier date codes. The date of final withdrawal is not recorded.

B A Widow and her Friends
SCENES/TITLES
1 'She contemplates the cloister.'
2 'She decides to die in spite of Dr. Bottles.'
3 'She finds that exercise does not improve her spirits.'
4 'Miss Babbles, the Authoress, calls and reads aloud.'
5 'She finds some consolation in her mirror.'
6 'A quiet dinner with Dr. Bottles, after which he reads aloud Miss Babbles' latest work.'
7 'A message from the outside world.'
8 'Some think that she has remained in retirement too long. (Others are surprised that she is about so soon).'
9 'She is the subject of more hostile criticism.'
10 'Mrs. Diggs is alarmed at discovering what she imagines to be a snare that threatens the safety of her only child. Mr. Diggs does

Gibson. Rack plates, Gibson Girl heads, with lovers' knots and hearts border

Gibson. Rack plates, Gibson Girl heads, with lovers' knots and hearts border

Gibson. Rack plates, *A Widow and Her Friends*, scenes B1 to B12, stylised foliate border

Gibson. Rack plates, *A Widow and Her Friends*, scenes B13 to B24, stylised foliate border

not share his wife's anxiety.'
11 'She looks for relief among some of the old ones. (A pile of books on the floor).'
12 'She longs for seclusion and decides to leave town for a milder climate. While preparing for the journey she comes across some old things that recall other days.'
13 'The day after arriving at her journey's end.'
14 'She goes into colors.'
15 'They go fishing.'
16 'Failing to find rest and quiet in the country she decides to return home.'
17 'Mr. Waddles arrives late and finds her card filled.'
18 'She becomes a trained nurse.'
19 'They take a morning run.'
20 'Miss Babbles brings a copy of a morning paper, and expresses her indignation and sympathy over a scurrilous article. Meanwhile other friends are calling upon the editor.'
21 'They go skating.'
22 'She goes to the fancy dress ball as "Juliet".'
23 'She is disturbed by a vision which appears to be herself.'
24 'And here, winning new friends and not losing the old ones, we leave her.'

Gibson. *Left to right, above* C6, C7, *centre* C13, C16, *below* C14, C15

Gibson. Vases, *left to right, above* C10, C1, C11, *below* C4, C2, C3

BORDERS
Stylised foliate.

COLOURWAYS
Black, or dark sepia, blue and white.

SHAPES
Rack plates only.

DATES
These designs were introduced in 1901. The date of withdrawal is not recorded although it was probably during World War I.
Note This series was pirated in the 1960s by another company. The fakes are badly printed and are easily discernible on close comparison with the originals.

C Mostly Golfing Scenes
SCENES/TITLES
1 'Golf—a good game for two'.
2 'Is a caddie always necessary?'
3 'Don't watch the player, keep your eye on the ball'.
4 'One difficulty of the game—keeping your eye on the ball'.
5 'Fore'.
6 'Who cares?'
7 'The girl he left behind him'.
8 'A little incident'.

9 'Wasting Time'.
10 'From 10 a.m. to 6.45 p.m. this dog has been kept out. Where is the S.P.C.A.?'
11 'The last day of summer'.
12 'Here it's Christmas and they began saying goodbye in August'.
13 'The susceptible rock'.
14 'Melting'.
15 'Love in a garden'.
16 'The Dog'.

PATTERN NUMBERS
E2766, E2827.

COLOURWAYS
Polychrome, sepia, black, blue.

SHAPES
Pin tray, small vases (not in shape guide).

DATES
This series was introduced in 1904. The date of withdrawal is not recorded although it was probably during World War I.

Greenaway

Kate Greenaway (1846–1901), the English artist and book illustrator, revolutionised both children's books and children's fashions at the end of the 19th century. The Doulton series is based on her almanack of 1884 which records the events she remembered, famous days, famous births and famous deaths. Doulton also produce a range of figures based on Kate Greenaway designs.

Almanack plates

SCENES/TITLES
 1 Aquarius: The Water Bearer, January
 2 Pisces: The Fishes, February
 3 Aries: The Ram, March
 4 Taurus: The Bull, April

 5 Gemini: The Twins, May
 6 Cancer: The Crab, June
 7 Leo: The Lion, July
 8 Virgo: The Virgin, August
 9 Libra: The Balance, September
 10 Scorpio: The Scorpion, October
 11 Sagittarius: The Archer, November
 12 Capricornus: The Goat, December

SHAPES
Rack plates.

DATES
This series was introduced in 1978 and is still in production.

SPECIAL BACKSTAMP

Greenaway. Rack plate 6 Cancer, with special backstamp

Greenaway. Rack plate 7 Leo, with special backstamp

Jansson

Augustus L. Jansson (1890–?) was an American painter based in West Somerville, Massachusetts. Three of his designs of playing card characters featured on Doulton rack plates and jugs. Wedgwood also produced a series of similar designs. Twelve different quotations are recorded on plates copyrighted in 1909.

SCENES/TITLES

1 'Ye King of Hearts is true love's king
   He joins or parts gives rue or ring'
2 'Ye Queen of Hearts we all do know
   She won our hearts long years ago'
3 'Ye Knave of Hearts is one so base
   He'll shock a maid and flush her face'

PATTERN NUMBERS

D3655, D3657, D3665, D3969.

BORDERS

Stylised flower and fluted, gadroon.

COLOURWAYS

Red, black and yellow on light background.
Red and white on black background.

SHAPES

Rack plates, Tudor jug.

DATES

These designs were introduced in 1913 and were in production until about 1932.

Jansson. Jug 1

Jansson. Rack plate 3

Souter

David Henry Souter (1862–1935) illustrator and writer was born and trained in Britain but emigrated to Australia in his early twenties. There he joined the staff of the Sydney current affairs magazine *The Bulletin* and rapidly became known throughout that continent for his Art Nouveau style illustration of cats. His popular character *Kateroo* was adapted to model form by Doulton as well as featuring on series ware.

A
SCENES/TITLES

1 'The Tiff'
2 'The Honeymoon'
3 'O Perfect Love'
4 'The Lovers'
5 'The Gay Bachelor'
6 'The Wedding Tour'

Souter. Rack plates with Art Nouveau border,
left to right, above A5, A1, A4, *below* A6, A2, A3

Souter. Plates with cellular borders, showing
cat characters

PATTERN NUMBERS
D2504, D2666, D3407.

BORDERS
Art Nouveau, cellular.

COLOURWAYS
Polychrome, green and white.

SHAPES
Rack plates.

B

SCENES/TITLES
1 'Trust not him that seems a saint'
2 'East West Hame's Best'
3 'Here we go round the Mulberry Bush'
4 'Better alone than in bad company'
5 'Be content the sea hath fish enough'
6 'Pussy cat which . . .' (quote not completely
  legible on only example known)

PATTERN NUMBERS
D2498, D2591, D3953, D4153, E3236.

CHARACTERS
A variety of cat characters in different
combinations feature in these scenes; front

Souter. *Left* B4, *right* cat characters

Souter. *Left* B3, *right* B5

Souter. C1

Souter. C2

view seated cat, back view seated cat, profile seated cat, prowling cat, prowling cat tail erect, stalking cat, poised-to-pounce cat, lying cat, lying cat legs outstretched.

BORDERS
Cat, mouse, ivy wall, cellular, or none.

COLOURWAYS
Polychrome, Celadon ware, Holbein glaze.

SHAPES
Rack plates, spittoon, Ball teapot, Windmill coffee pot, Empire teacup and saucer, Nelson teacup and saucer.
Vase numbers 1032A, 7040B, 7338A.

C
SCENES/TITLES
1 'God bless the cat that breaks the crocks
In pieces very small
For things like that are good for trade and benefit us all'.

2 'The object which excites our love
May neighbours angry passion move
Therefore do not complain if he
May not see eye to eye with thee.
Dash that Tom, Is that you Tom?'

PATTERN NUMBERS
D3066, E3793.

SHAPES
Pin trays, Tavern jug.

DATES
All Souter series were introduced c1905 and expanded greatly before the 1914–18 war. All appear to have been withdrawn by 1939.

Aeronautical scenes. *Left*, spittoon
1, 2, *right* rack plate with oriental
border, 6, 4

Aeronautical scenes. Rack plates,
left to right, 4, 3, 7, 3, 5, 4

Historical Characters and Events

Aeronautical Scenes

This series appears to have been inspired by the first International Air Race meeting held at Rheims in August 1909. The background on some of the plates includes a racecourse and stand which suggest the racecourse at Rheims where the meeting was held. All except one of the aircraft depicted on Doulton wares are known to have flown at this event and competed for prizes donated by the champagne industry.

SCENES/TITLES
1 Cody
2 Antoinette
3 Wright type A (two versions)
4 Standard Voisin
5 Artist's fantasy which resembles the De-Dion Bouton
6 Astra airship
7 Lebaudy airship
8 Balloons
Note Two or three of the above were used on each item.

PATTERN NUMBERS
D3205.

BORDER
Oriental or no border.

SHAPES
Rack plates, Scotia jug and spittoon.

DATES
This series was introduced in 1909 and withdrawn by 1914.

Authors and Inns

This series features well-known authors outside inns with which they are connected. Chaucer's pilgrims met at the Tabard Inn prior to journeying to Canterbury; Goldsmith wrote The Vicar of Wakefield at his house near Ye Rosemary Inn and Sir Walter Raleigh visited Ye Queens Head in Old Islington.

SCENES/TITLES
1 Chaucer in front of 'Ye Tabard Southwark'.
'Be felle that in that season on a day
In Southwark at the tabard as I lay
Redy to wander on my pilgrimage
To Canterbury with devoute courage.
Chaucer'.
2 Goldsmith in front of 'Ye Rosemary Branch Inn and Oliver Goldsmith's House in which the Vicar of Wakefield was written'.
3 Raleigh in front of 'Ye Queens Head in old Islington, The resort of Queen Elizabeth, Raleigh, Earl of Essex and etc.'
4 The Queens Head, Islington also features with no character, inscribed
'Whoe'er has travelled life's dull round
Where'er his stages may have been
I ay sigh to think he still has found
The warmest welcome at an inn. Shenstone'.

PATTERN NUMBERS
D2079, D3602, D3603, D3624.

COLOURWAYS
Polychrome, blue and white, sepia.

SHAPES
Rack plates, jugs (not in shape guide).

DATES
The inns with famous characters first made their appearance in 1904 but there is no record of their withdrawal date. The 'Queen's Head' plates were introduced in 1912.

Opposite top left. Authors and Inns. 1

Opposite far left. Authors and Inns. 2

Opposite right. Authors and Inns. Jug 3

The Bayeux Tapestry

This embroidery on linen was created at the request of Bishop Odo, half-brother to William the Conqueror. Over 200 feet long, it relates the story of the Norman conquest of England in 1066. It can be seen in its own museum in Bayeux, Normandy.

SCENES/TITLES

1 William ordering his messenger to ransom Harold. 'Venit: Nuntius Ad Wil Gelmum Ducem'
2 'Coronation of Harold'. 'Hic Re Sidet Harold Rex An Glorium Stignant Archiv. Eps'
3 Spying the comet. 'Isti mirant stella'
4 Ship at sea. 'Landing at Pevensey'
5 Odo, Robert and William deciding to build a fort. 'Odo: Eps Rotbert Willelm'
6 'Death of Harold'

Note Various combat scenes from the tapestry appear alone or as part of a frieze on bowls, plates, etc. The quotations do not always appear on the image, particularly on smaller items.

PATTERN NUMBERS
D2873.

BORDERS
Battle frieze, or castle and mythical beasts.

SHAPES
Rack plates, Lennox flower bowl, round salad bowl, Marcella tobacco jar, Concord jug, Teniers jug, Rheims teacup and saucer, Pelican trinket set, Mayfair toilet set, Loving cup 7352.
Vase numbers 6061, 7013, 7014, 7016, 7040, 7346, 7348, 7383, 7384, 7385, 7432, 7444, 7465, 7531.

DATES
The series was introduced in 1907 and withdrawn around 1930.

SPECIAL BACKSTAMP

Below: Bayeux Tapesty. *Left to right*, 1, 4, 3 (advertising photograph)

Bayeux Tapestry. Rack plates, *left to right* 6, 4, 5

Bayeux Tapestry. Jugs,
left to right 6, 2

Castles & Churches

Britain is rich in old buildings, each with its
own history and legends. *Arundel Castle*, seat
of the Dukes of Norfolk started as a Norman
keep. Extensively restored in the 1890s it is
everyone's ideal of a mediaeval castle.
According to tradition, *St Martin's Abbey*,
better known as Battle Abbey, was built by
William the Conqueror on the hilltop where
Harold died. *Bodiam Castle*, once a magnificent
fortress, is now a hollow shell surrounded by
a beautiful lilied moat. *Cawdor Castle*, a
square tower near Inverness is best-remembered
for its associations with Macbeth. *Croydon
Church*, with its 15th century tower contains
the tombs of six Archbishops of Canterbury
while *Fountains Abbey*, in Yorkshire, founded
by Benedictine monks in 1132-3 is a well-
preserved ruin. *Hurstmonceaux Castle*, dating
from the 15th century, now houses the Royal
Observatory. *Pembroke Castle* is one of the
largest Norman castles, surrounded on three
sides by water while *Rochester Castle* has the
finest Norman keep in Southern England.
Dryburgh Abbey, on the Scottish border, contains
the tomb of Sir Walter Scott in *St Mary's Aisle*.
Muckross Abbey is a 15th century ruin in the
grounds of an estate in Killarney lake district,
County Kerry. *Warwick Castle* is one of the few
mediaeval fortresses continually occupied and
Windsor Castle founded by William I is still the
residence of the Royal Family.

Castles
SCENES/TITLES
1. Arundel Castle. D3671, D4505
2. Bodiam Castle (two versions). D3471,
   D3491, D3691, D4391, D4504
3. Cawdor Castle. D5413
4. Hurstmonceaux Castle. D3471
5. Pembroke Castle. D3599, D3610, D4643,
   D4911
6. Rochester Castle (three versions). D4728,
   D5995, D6112, D6308,
7. Warwick Castle. D4643, H2941
8. Windsor Castle. H2948

Churches
SCENES/TITLES
9. Battle Abbey. D3471
10. Croydon Church. No pattern number
11. Fountains Abbey. D4358
12. Muckross Abbey. D2654
13. St Mary's Aisle, Dryburgh. D5412, D5413

Note Miscellaneous buildings have also been
noted under the following pattern numbers:
E7239, V2352, D3425, D3426, D5433,
TC1092, 1095.

PATTERN NUMBERS
Arranged above for easier reference.

COLOURWAYS
Polychrome, blue and white, sepia, Holbein
glaze.

Castles & Churches. Rack plates, *left to right*, *above* 11, 8, 3, *below* 1, 9, 4

Castles & Churches. Rack plates, *left to right*, *above* 6 (3 versions), *below* 2 (2 versions), 5

SHAPES
Rack plates, Concord jug, Lennox flower bowl, celery tray.

DATES

The earliest castle or church scene recorded on Series ware was in the *Pottery Gazette* of March 1908 which described them as 'exquisite views of English cathedrals by W. Nunn'. So far none of these items have been found. From 1911 onwards a number of castles and churches were depicted on rack plates and this trend continued until the early 1950s.

Eglington Tournament

Held in 1839 by the 13th Earl of Eglington at Eglington Castle in Ayrshire as a reaction to the simplicity of Victoria's coronation, the medieval tournament, complete with Queen of Beauty, knights in armour, jousting and other Gothic activities, was watched by 100,000 people. Unfortunately violent rainstorms ruined the occasion.

SCENES/TITLES
1 The Queen on horseback with attendants
2 A knight in procession with foot soldiers
3 Two knights addressing a foot soldier
4 Queen bestowing favour to saluting knights
5 Marshall signalling knights to be ready
6 Knights charging with lances
7 Knights in sword combat

Eglington Tournament. *Left to right, above* 1, 7, 6, *below* 3, 2, 5, 4

PATTERN NUMBERS
D1425, D1455, D1461, D1462, D1496, D1514, D1776, D2039, D2792, D2793, D2794, D3054, D3055.

BORDERS
Laurel leaf and/or gadroons.

COLOURWAYS
Polychrome, sepia and green, blue and white,

Eglington Tournament. *Left to right*, jug 2, rack plate 7 with gadroon border, jug 6 with laurel leaf and gadroon border blue and pink, green and yellow, Whieldon ware, Holbein glaze.

SHAPES
Rack plates, Concord jug, Castle jug, Regent fern bowl.

DATES
The series was introduced in 1902 and the range of items increased in 1908. It was completely withdrawn in 1928.

Famous Sailing Ships

Many famous sailing ships are represented in this embossed series, which reflects the British fascination with the sea.

Fighting Ships: *Henri Grace à Dieu*, launched in 1515, was the largest ship of her day and flagship of Henry VIII; Lord Howard's flagship against the Spanish Armada in 1588 was the *Ark Royal*, while Sir Francis Drake captained the *Revenge* which later, under Sir Richard Grenville, fought 53 Spanish ships before an honourable surrender; the Napoleonic Wars saw the *Active* and the *Hydra* in action as well as the *Victory*, Nelson's flagship at Trafalgar, 1805; finally, the *Acorn* under Commander Adams played a large part in destroying the slave-traders of the 1840s. **Exploration:** John Cabot searched for the North-West passage to the Indies in the *Matthew*, 1497; the *Golden Hind* was the first English ship to circumnavigate the globe, under Drake, 1577–80; Abel Tasman discovered Tasmania in the *Heemskerck* in 1642 and a hundred years later Cook sailed to the Pacific and Australasia in the *Endeavour*, 1768–72, followed by Captain Phillips in *Sirius* who founded Sydney in 1788; the same year in which the *Bounty*, taking bread-fruit from the Pacific to the West-Indies, under William Bligh, suffered her infamous mutiny. **Merchantmen:** the *East Indiaman* is typical of the ships of the East India Company which monopolised trade to the East in the late 18th century; later came the clippers, such as *Sussex*, 1852, built to carry tea and wool as quickly as possible; the *Cutty Sark*, 1863, held

the record for a day's sailing of 363 nautical miles; lastly the *Fernande* was a racing schooner which won the Queen's vase at Plymouth in 1847.

SCENES/TITLES
1 'HMS Victory'
2 'Sirius'
3 'Cutty Sark'
4 'Active'
5 'Acorn'
6 'Matthew'
7 'Revenge'
8 'Henri Grace à Dieu'
9 'HMS Bounty'
10 'Golden Hind'
11 'Hydra'
12 'Sussex'
13 'Fernande'
14 'Heemskerck'
15 'Endeavour'
16 'Ark Royal'
17 'East Indiaman'

PATTERN NUMBERS
D5957.

SHAPES
A variety of specially moulded shapes (not featured in the shape guide).

DATES
The series was introduced in 1938 and withdrawn about twenty years later.

SPECIAL BACKSTAMP

Famous Sailing Ships.
Selection of wares

Below: Famous Sailing
Ships. Selection of wares

Historic Towns

London, a great city since Roman times, has a wealth of historic sites. *Smithfield*, its huge meat market erected in 1867, was an execution site from the 12th century. Close by are *St Bartholomew's the Great*, oldest Norman church in London (1123) and *Pie Corner*, where the Great Fire of 1666 was (incorrectly) thought to have ended. Following the fire, Sir Christopher Wren rebuilt *St Paul's Cathedral* (1675–1710) and *Temple Bar*, a triple gateway marking the boundary of the cities of London and Westminster, dismantled in 1878, which

would have been known to *Dr Samuel Johnson* (1709–84) who lived near *Fleet St*. *St Dunstan's*, an unusual octagonal church rebuilt in 1829, houses a 'striking jacks' clock of 1671. At *Clerkenwell* is *St John's Gate*, 1504, once the main entrance to the priory of the order of the Hospital of *St John of Jerusalem*, better known as the Knights Hospitallers. The priory, founded in 1148 was dissolved during the Reformation (1559) by Henry VIII who lived in *Hampton Court*, built originally for Cardinal Wolsey. On Highgate Hill is the

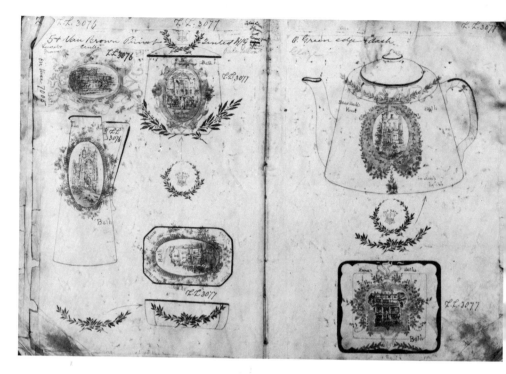

Whittington stone, marking where Dick Whittington supposedly sat when he heard the Bow Bells calling him back to London. *Bath*, once a Roman town, is now famous for the architecture of Beau Nash and Ralph Allen's sham Gothic Castle. *Bristol* is one of England's leading and most elegant seaports, particularly of the 17th and 18th centuries. Past residents include explorer Sebastian Cabot, philanthropist Edward Colston and poet Thomas Chatterton. The county town of Devon, *Exeter* has long been the market centre for the surrounding countryside while *Winchester*, the Saxon capital of Wessex, is best-known for its association with Alfred the Great who was crowned there.

A Old London
SCENES/TITLES
1 'Sir Richard Whittington, Thrice Lord Mayor of London'.
2 'Whittington's Stone in 1820'.
3 'The Monastery of St. John of Jerusalem, Clerkenwell'.
4 'Another part of the monastery'.
5 'Pie Corner where the great fire ended, Smithfield'.

6 'Pie Corner, The Watchman'.
7 'The Watchman'.
8 'Old Smithfields Market'.
9 'St. Bartholomew the Great, Smithfields'.
10 Another view of St. Bartholomews.
11 'Place of Execution, Old Smithfield'.
12 'Dr. Johnson. Let us take a walk down Fleet St.'
13 'Temple Bar in Johnson's Time'.
14 'The Palace of Cardinal Wolsey and King Henry VIII'.
15 'Fleet St, The Clock of Old St. Dunstan's'.
16 'St. Pauls from Old Smithfield Market'.
17 'St. John's Gate—still standing'.
18 'David Garrick St. John's Gate, Clerkenwell. Scene of his first performance in London.'
Note Various combinations of these scenes appear on each item.

PATTERN NUMBERS
D2104, D2105, D2351, D2557.

COLOURWAYS
Polychrome, sepia, Whieldon ware.

SHAPES
Vase number 7018.

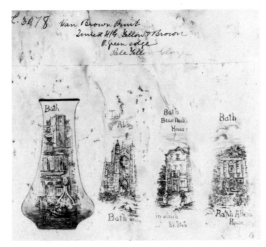

Historic Towns. *Left to right* B6, B4, B5, B7

Opposite: Historic Towns. *Left page, above* B4, B3, *below* B4, B5, *right page, above* B5, *below* B2

Historic Towns, Bath. *Above* B1, *below* B6

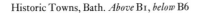

DATES
This series was introduced in 1904 with additions being made until 1906. The date of withdrawal is not recorded.

DESIGNER
W. Nunn.

SPECIAL BACKSTAMP

B Old Bath
SCENES/TITLES
1 'Sham Castle'.
2 'Roman Baths'.
3 'Pump Room'.
4 'The Abbey'.
5 'Beau Nash's House in which he died'.
6 'Roman Spring'.
7 'Ralph Allen's House'.

BORDERS
Various cartouches with flowers.

SHAPES
Virginia tobacco jar, Breda tea service, Pelican comb tray, pin trays and ashtrays, Jug 6061. Vase numbers 7012, 7023.

DATES
In production c1905.

DESIGNER
W. Nunn.

SPECIAL BACKSTAMP

C Old Bristol
SCENES/TITLES
1 'Sebastian Cabot'.
2 'Bristol Cathedral'.
3 'Christmas Steps'.
4 'Bristol Docks'.
5 'The Bridge', Green's Dock.
6 'St. Augustine's Gate'.
7 'St. Peter's Hospital'.
8 'Another view of St. Peter's Hospital where Chatterton used to walk and read his poems'.
9 'E. Colston philanthropist at the gateway of St. Bartholomews Hospital'.
10 'Temple Church'.
11 'Pie Poudre Court'.
12 'Old Market Street'.
13 'Shakespeare Inn'.

Historic Towns. *Above* C1, C2, *below* C3, C4, *left to right* C7, C8, C6, C5.

Historic Towns. *Above* D1, D2, *below* D1, D3

Historic Towns. *First column* A4, A17, *second column* A1, A5, A9, A3, A11, *third column* A2, A16, A7, A9, A8, *fourth column* A6, A12, A13, A14, A15

PATTERN NUMBERS
No record.

SHAPES
Miniature vases.

DATES
In production c1905.

DESIGNER
W. Nunn.

D Old Exeter
SCENES/TITLES
1 'The Cathedral'
2 'Exeter in Fore St'
3 'The Guildhall'
4 'The Castle'

PATTERN NUMBERS
No record.

Below Historic Towns,
vase E4, jug A18

SHAPES
Rheims teacup and saucer, Concord jug,
Loving cup 7058.
Vase number 7023.

DATES
In production c1905.

DESIGNER
W. Nunn.

E Old Winchester
SCENES/TITLES
1 'The Cathedral'
2 'The Westgate'
3 'St. Cross Church'
4 'St. Cross'

PATTERN NUMBERS
Not recorded.

SHAPES
Vase number 7013.

DATES
In production c1905.

SPECIAL BACKSTAMP

Note: It is possible that other towns and cities
may have featured in this series.

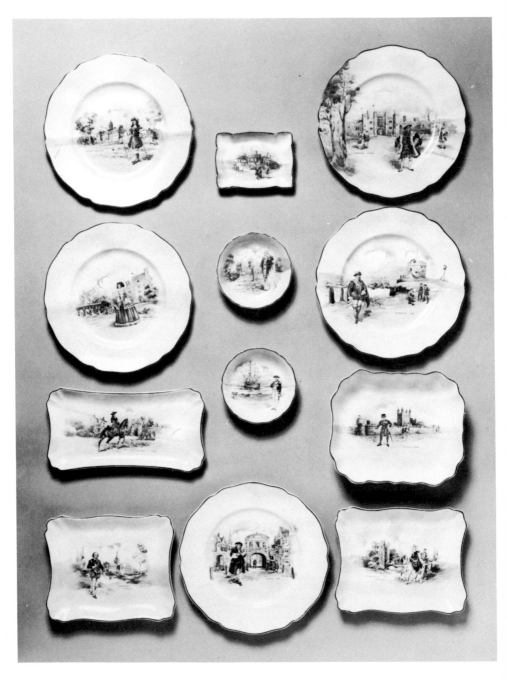

Historic England. *Left column* 2, 10, 7, 11, *centre column* 13, 3, 8, 5, *right column* 1, 4, 9, 6

Historic England

Throughout history famous people have always been linked with particular places, as illustrated in this series. *Bootham Bar* is one of the gateways to York where *Dick Turpin* the notorious highwayman was hung in 1739. *Archbishop Thomas à Becket* was murdered in *Canterbury Cathedral* by Henry II in 1170 and later canonized. *Chelsea Hospital* was founded by *Charles II* (1630–85) for veteran and invalid soldiers—about 500 pensioners are still boarded there. *Haddon Hall,* seat of the dukes of Rutland saw the elopement of *Dorothy Vernon* with John Manners during her sister's wedding party. *Hampton Court,* on the river Thames, was built by Cardinal Wolsey (1514) and passed to *Henry VIII* who used it as his royal residence. *Kenilworth Castle* was the home of Robert Dudley, Earl of Leicester, the favourite of *Elizabeth I.* According to tradition, *Sir Francis Drake* was playing bowls at *Plymouth Hoe* when the Spanish Armada was sighted in 1588—and insisted on finishing his game before sailing. *William Shakespeare* was buried in the *Holy Trinity Church* in *Stratford* in 1616, and the writer *Dr Johnson* (1709–84) spent much time in London around *Temple Bar* the gateway between the cities of London and Westminster, opposite the Law Courts. The *Beefeaters* at the *Tower of London,* originally the private guard of Henry VII, now have only ceremonial duties. The *Victory,* on which *Nelson* lost his life in 1805 can still be visited at Portsmouth Dock. *Robin Hood,* the popular outlaw, fought his adversary the Sheriff at *Nottingham Castle.*

SCENES/TITLES
1 'Henry VIII at Hampton Court'
2 'Charles II at Chelsea Hospital'
3 'Thomas à Becket at Canterbury Cathedral'
4 'Sir Francis Drake at Plymouth Hoe'
5 'Dr. Johnson at Temple Bar'
6 'Queen Elizabeth at Kenilworth Castle'
7 'Dick Turpin at Bootham Bar, York'
8 'Lord Nelson with the Victory'
9 'Beefeaters at the Tower of London'
10 'Dorothy Vernon at Haddon Hall'
11 'Shakespeare at Stratford Church'
12 'Robin Hood at Nottingham Castle'
13 Sedan chair scene (no details recorded)

PATTERN NUMBERS
D5940.

SHAPES
Rack plates, Dame tea service, New Barton jug, various shaped dishes (not featured in the shape guide).

DATES
This series was introduced in 1938 and withdrawn about 1952.

DESIGNER
M.F.

SPECIAL BACKSTAMP

Doctor Johnson

Samuel Johnson (1709–84), the son of a country bookseller, was one of England's leading literary figures best known as the compiler of the first major dictionary of the English language. He founded a club which included painter Joshua Reynolds, philosopher Edmund Burke, and poet Oliver Goldsmith and met at various coffee-houses and inns, including the *Cheshire Cheese,* which still stands in Fleet Street, London.

SCENES/TITLES
1 'Dr. Johnson at the Cheshire Cheese 1776–84.'

PATTERN NUMBERS
D3123, D5910, D6377.

BORDERS
Inscription as above or no border.

COLOURWAYS
Polychrome, sepia.

SHAPES
Rack plates, chop dish.

DATES
The design with the inscription border was introduced in 1909 and remained in production until 1938. In that year a new design with a more extensive background was introduced, being withdrawn in 1952. An isolated chop dish was also produced in 1952.

Dr Johnson. *Left* rack plate with inscription border, *centre* chop dish, *right* rack plate with plain border

Nautical History

A maritime nation, Britain has a long tradition of respecting naval achievement, as shown by the introduction of this series. *Samuel de Champlain*, c1507–35, founded Quebec and Port Royal, laying the basis for French claims to Canada, while *Sir Martin Frobisher*, c1535–94 discovered Frobisher Bay but failed to find a North-West passage to the Indies. *Sir Walter Raleigh* introduced tobacco and potatoes to England from America and fought the Spanish with *Sir Francis Drake* who, in the Golden Hind, became the first Englishman to sail around the world. During the Napoleonic wars, Admiral Jervis's important victory over the Spanish off Cape St Vincent (1797) led to his being created *Earl of St Vincent*. During that engagement he was supported by Horatio Nelson, later *Admiral Lord Nelson* who went on to victories at Copenhagen and Trafalgar (1805). There are two naval actions which stand out in English history. The *Spanish Armada* (1588), an invasion force led by the Duke of Medina Sidonia, was defeated by the smaller, more manoeuvrable English ships under Lord Howard and Drake. At the *Battle of Trafalgar*, 1805, Admiral Nelson was mortally wounded when his fleet decisively beat the French under Villeneuve.

A

SCENES/TITLES
1 Battle of Trafalgar
2 Spanish Armada

PATTERN NUMBERS
D3049, D3052, D3086, D3101.

BORDERS
Frieze of galleons.

COLOURWAYS
Polychrome, sepia and yellow, blue and white.

Nautical History, Rack plates, *left to right*, *above* B1, A1, B3, *below* B4, A2, B2

SHAPES
Rack plates.

DATES
These designs were introduced in 1908 and withdrawn by 1928.

B
SCENES/TITLES
1 Sir Walter Raleigh
2 Sir Francis Drake
3 Sir Martin Frobisher (mis-spelt Forbisher on Doulton items)
4 Samuel de Champlain

PATTERN NUMBERS
D2787, D2788, D2810, D3053, D3939, D3940, D3941, D4843, D4849, D4852.

BORDERS
Galleons and seagulls, basket type.

Nautical History. Rack plates, *above* C2, *below* C1

95

COLOURWAYS
Polychrome, blue and white, green and yellow,
Holbein glaze.

SHAPES
Rack plates, Octagon plates, sandwich plate,
Armada jug.

DATES
These designs were introduced in 1907 and
were in production with modifications to
borders and colourways in subsequent editions
until 1955.
Note See *Authors and Inns* for portrait of
Raleigh at the Queens Head, Islington.

C
SCENES/TITLES
1 Admiral Lord Nelson
2 The Earl of St Vincent

PATTERN NUMBERS
D3514.

SHAPES
Rack plates, Tudor jug.

DATES
These designs were introduced in 1911 and
were probably withdrawn with series A by
1928.

Old English Inns

England is full of old inns which have
continued to refresh travellers through the
centuries. The *Bears Head, Brereton*, a
half-timbered house dating from 1615 has vast
ranges of redbrick stables from the days of
post-chaises. *The Bell, Hurley*, has stood in a
quiet village on the Thames for 500 years,
while the *Cat and Fiddle* at *Hinton Admiral*
was used by smugglers off-loading goods
brought up from Christchurch. The *Fighting
Cocks, St Albans*, is one of England's oldest
inns, rebuilt in 1600 on mediaeval foundations.
The *Kings Head, Chigwell* was used by Dickens
as the model for the Maypole in Barnaby
Rudge and the *Leather Bottle, Cobham*,
features in The Pickwick Papers. *The Peacock,
Rowsley*, was once the Dower house of Haddon
Hall, seat of the Dukes of Rutland while the

Old English Inns. *Top to bottom* 6, 1, 3, 2

Old English
Inns. *Left to right*
5, 4, 7, 8

Old Moreton Hall

Royal Oak, Winsford, is a picturesque thatched inn near the prehistoric Tarr Steps Bridge.

SCENES/TITLES
1 'The Leather Bottle, Cobham'.
2 'The Bear's Head, Brereton'.
3 'The Bell, Hurley'.
4 'The Fighting Cocks, St. Albans'.
5 'The Royal Oak, Winsford, Somerset'.
6 'The Peacock, Rowsley'.
7 'The Kings Head, Chigwell'.
8 'The Cat and the Fiddle, Hinton Admiral'.

PATTERN NUMBERS
D6072, V2353 (china version).

BORDERS
Oak leaf.

SHAPES
Rack plates, Dame tea service.

DATES
This series was introduced in 1939 in earthenware, with a bone china version added in 1947. It was completely withdrawn by 1958.

Little Moreton Hall, Cheshire, is surely the most picturesque half-timbered house in the country. It was built during the sixteenth century although there were later additions. Queen Elizabeth I visited the Hall in 1589, and the Doulton designs illustrate this event. The Hall is only a few miles north of the Staffordshire Potteries, where the Doulton Burslem factory is located.

SCENES/TITLES
1 The Squire and his lady awaiting Queen Elizabeth's arrival in a sedan chair
2 The Squire and his lady receiving Queen Elizabeth and her attendants at the entrance
3 The Squire in the entrance
4 The Squire receiving Queen Elizabeth and a small procession with jester
5 The Squire taking Queen Elizabeth's hand
6 The Squire and his lady watching guests dancing
7 The Squire, his lady and their daughter with a courtier in front of the house
8 Two courtiers strolling past the house.
9 A man in the stocks
Note On some items, particularly bowls, a frieze is composed of a combination of certain scenes.

PATTERN NUMBERS
D3822, D3858.

BORDERS
Acanthus leaves and/or scenes of the hall.

COLOURWAYS
Polychrome, blue and white, sepia.

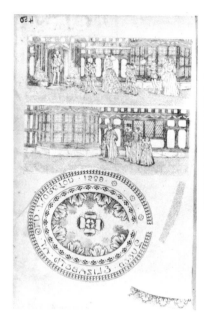

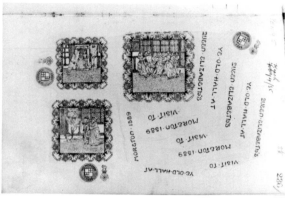

Left: Old Moreton Hall. *Above* 4, *below* 7

Old Moreton Hall. *Above* 2, 6, *below* 8, special backstamp

Below: Old Moreton Hall. *Left* 1, *right* 5

SHAPES
Rack plates, stein, Lennox flower bowl, Ascot cheese dish, round salad bowl, round Leeds fruit dish, porridge plate, Rex mug, Pelican trinket set, Dale tea service, Marcella tobacco jar, safety match stand, Ancestor ashtray, Regent fern pot, hair tidy, tea caddy, celery tray, candlestick 7277, Loving cup 7058. Shaped dishes (not featured in shape guide).

DATES
This series was introduced in 1915 and withdrawn in 1933.

SPECIAL BACKSTAMP

St George

Originally a Palestinian soldier martyred in Asia Minor, St George is generally represented slaying a dragon. His cult was brought to England by the Crusaders and he became the patron Saint. He was recently decanonized by the Roman Catholic church.

SCENES/TITLES
1 St George on horseback brandishing his his sword
2 St George on horseback galloping

PATTERN NUMBERS
D2965, D5108, D5109, D5110, D5111.

BORDER
Dead dragon.

COLOURWAYS
Blue and orange, green and yellow, blue and yellow and probably others.

SHAPES
Rack plates.

DATES
The design was introduced in 1908, and a wide range of colourways made their appearance in 1931 and were withdrawn around 1945.

St George. Rack plate 1

Stately Plates

Eight famous stately homes are depicted in this series. *Warwick Castle* is one of the few medieval castles in this country still inhabited. *Blenheim Palace*, which was designed by Vanbrugh in the early 18th century, boasts magnificent grounds laid out by Capability Brown. *Woburn Abbey*, the home of the Russell family, is surrounded by 3,000 acres of park stocked with some of the rarest wild animals in private hands. *Castle Howard* is another Vanbrugh masterpiece. *Longleat House*, the home of the Marquesses of Bath for four centuries, is now well known for the safari park in its grounds. *Scone Palace*, with its castellated towers, was erected in 1803 on the site of an ancient abbey founded by King Kenneth I of Scotland. *Beaulieu Abbey*, founded by King John as a Cistercian Abbey in 1204, is now the home of the National Motor Museum. *Harewood House* was designed by Robert Adam and the grounds are another example of Capability Brown's consummate skill.

SCENES/TITLES
1 Warwick Castle, Warwickshire
2 Blenheim Palace, Oxfordshire
3 Woburn Abbey, Bedfordshire
4 Castle Howard, Yorkshire
5 Longleat House, Wiltshire
6 Scone Palace, Perthshire
7 Beaulieu Abbey, Hampshire
8 Harewood House, Yorkshire

SHAPES
Rack plates.

DATES
This series was introduced in 1977 and withdrawn in the following year.

DESIGNER
Original illustrations by Reginald Johnson.

Photograph not available.

World War I 1914-1918

Doulton celebrated the end of the Great War with several themes, *Tipperary*, after the popular marching-song of the troops, and *Britannia-Victory in Peace*. Other series illustrated the *Women's Auxiliary Army Corps* and the warship *HMS Lion*, Admiral Beatty's flagship at the Battle of Jutland.

A

SCENES/TITLES
'Victory and Peace. Great Britain and her glorious colonies, America, France, Italy, Belgium, Japan, Portugal, Montenegro, Serbia and Roumania'.

PATTERN NUMBERS
Not recorded.

SHAPES
Rack plates, beakers.

DATES
1919.

B

SCENES/TITLES
'Its a long way to Tipperary Its a long way to go'. Soldier holding bayonet with Union Jack.

PATTERN NUMBERS
D3838, D3945.

BORDERS
Stylised foliate in black and red.

SHAPES
Rack plates, Corinth jug.

DATES
This design was introduced in 1915 and was in production until shortly after the end of the First World War.

C A Waac's Match

SCENES/TITLES
1 A 'Waac' with a handsome Australian soldier
2 A 'Waac' with a lanky British soldier

World War I. Rack plates, *left to right* D, B, A

PATTERN NUMBERS
H797.

SHAPES
Small plate, probably match strikers.

DATES
1919.

D
SCENES/TITLES
'HMS Lion 1914–18 Our Glorious Navy whose . . . has held the seas for Britain. (Title not completely legible on only example known).

PATTERN NUMBERS
Not recorded.

COLOURWAYS
Blue and white.

SHAPES
Large rack plates.

DATES
This design was introduced around 1916 and withdrawn by 1920.

World War I. *Left* C1, *right* C2

Pattern and Code Numbers & Date Guide

The following tables of numbers indicate the approximate periods when the relevant patterns so numbered were first *introduced*. Many patterns were in production over a number of years, carrying the same pattern number, and so the numbers cannot be used to establish the date of manufacture. This can be established either from the style of the backstamps, or from the impressed date code if present—normally the last two figures of the year preceded by a number indicating the month, for example 10.08 means a manufacturing date of October 1908. However, unless date codes are present, it is generally impossible to establish precise dates of manufacture for Series wares.

In the tables below, A and D numbers indicate earthenware patterns, while E and H were used for fine china.

A Numbers

Pattern number	Date of introduction
1 – 6882	c. 1881 – 1892
6883 – 7467	1893
7468 – 8084	1894
8085 – 8592	1895
8593 – 9144	1896
9145 – 9617	1897
9618 – 10000	1898

D Numbers

Pattern number	Date of introduction
1 – 339	1899
340 – 769	1900
770 – 1137	1901
1138 – 1495	1902
1496 – 1869	1903
1870 – 2161	1904
2162 – 2442	1905
2443 – 2723	1906
2724 – 2914	1907
2915 – 3079	1908
3080 – 3229	1909
3230 – 3374	1910
3375 – 3519	1911
3520 – 3635	1912
3636 – 3714	1913
3715 – 3821	1914
3822 – 3939	1915
3940 – 4074	1916 – 1918
4075 – 4143	1919 – 1920
4144 – 4230	1921 – 1922
4231 – 4360	·1923
4361 – 4470	1924
4471 – 4559	1925
4560 – 4659	1926
4660 – 4737	1927
4738 – 4822	1928
4823 – 4969	1929
4970 – 5069	1930

5070 – 5169	1931
5170 – 5230	1932
5231 – 5429	1933
5430 – 5520	1934
5521 – 5612	1935
5613 – 5749	1936
5750 – 5875	1937
5876 – 6009	1938
6010 – 6110	1939
6111 – 6285	1940 – 1948
6286 – 6390	1949 – 1952
6391 – 6408	1953
6409 – 6438	1954
6439 – 6454	1955
6455 – 6464	1956
6465 – 6492	1957
6493 – 6507	1958
6508 – 6547	1959
6548 – 6558	1960
6559 – 6567	1961
6568 – 6587	1962
6588 – 6596	1963
6597 – 6606	1964

E Numbers

Pattern number	Date of introduction
1 – 940	1901 – 1902
941 – 1950	1903
1951 – 3040	1904
3041 – 4054	1905 – 1906
4055 – 6015	1907 – 1910
6016 – 7683	1911
7684 – 8277	1912
8278 – 8933	1913
8934 – 9527	1914
9528 – 10000	1915

H Numbers

Pattern number	Date of introduction
1 – 359	1916
360 – 709	1917
710 – 759	1918
760 – 906	1919
907 – 1049	1920
1050 – 1179	1921
1180 – 1443	1922
1444 – 1812	1923
1813 – 2268	1924
2269 – 2649	1925
2650 – 3180	1926
3181 – 3599	1927
3600 – 3770	1928
3771 – 3909	1929
3910 – 4010	1930
4011 – 4099	1931
4100 – 4189	1932
4190 – 4240	1933
4241 – 4329	1934
4330 – 4425	1935
4426 – 4519	1936
4520 – 4609	1937
4610 – 4710	1938
4711 – 4821	1939 – 1942
4822 – 4849	1943 – 1946
4850 – 4906	1947 – 1952
4907 – 4930	1953
4931 – 4935	1954
4936 – 4941	1955
4942 – 4950	1956 – 1957
4951 – 4956	1958
4957 – 4959	1959
4960 – 4961	1960
4962 – 4964	1961
4965 – 4968	1962
4969 – 4975	1963

Shape Guide

The shapes illustrated in this guide include most of those on which Series ware patterns are commonly found. Each shape is identified by a name or number, and these should be used in conjunction with the list of recorded shapes included in each section in the book. Although wide ranging, this guide cannot hope to be comprehensive. It does not include, for example, bone china shapes and unusual early and late earthenware shapes. In addition, there may well be shapes in existence decorated with Series ware designs that are not recorded in the surviving pattern and shape books. The publisher of this book will be delighted to hear of any of these that come to light.

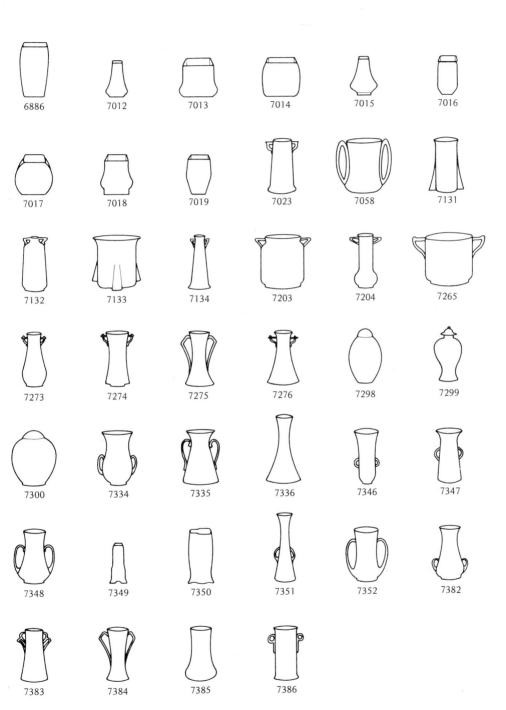

6886 7012 7013 7014 7015 7016

7017 7018 7019 7023 7058 7131

7132 7133 7134 7203 7204 7265

7273 7274 7275 7276 7298 7299

7300 7334 7335 7336 7346 7347

7348 7349 7350 7351 7352 7382

7383 7384 7385 7386

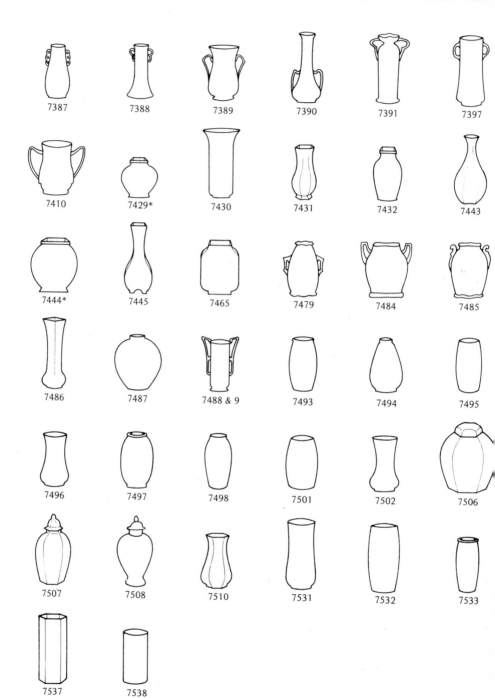

7387

7388

7389

7390

7391

7397

7410

7429*

7430

7431

7432

7443

7444*

7445

7465

7479

7484

7485

7486

7487

7488 & 9

7493

7494

7495

7496

7497

7498

7501

7502

7506

7507

7508

7510

7531

7532

7533

7537

7538

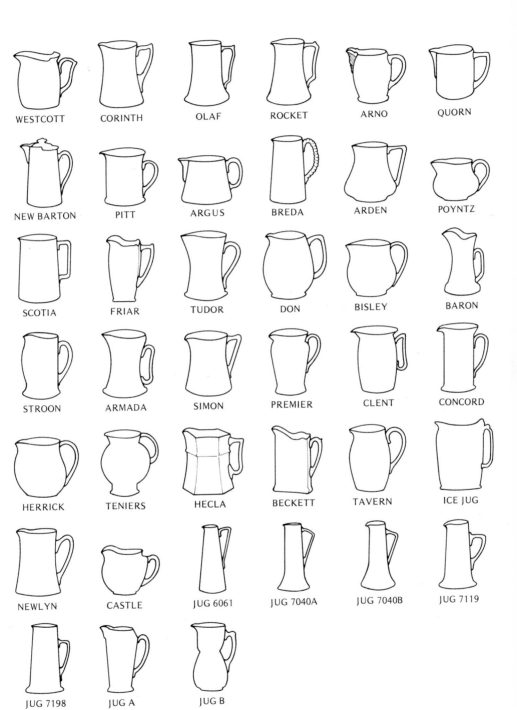

WESTCOTT   CORINTH   OLAF   ROCKET   ARNO   QUORN

NEW BARTON   PITT   ARGUS   BREDA   ARDEN   POYNTZ

SCOTIA   FRIAR   TUDOR   DON   BISLEY   BARON

STROON   ARMADA   SIMON   PREMIER   CLENT   CONCORD

HERRICK   TENIERS   HECLA   BECKETT   TAVERN   ICE JUG

NEWLYN   CASTLE   JUG 6061   JUG 7040A   JUG 7040B   JUG 7119

JUG 7198   JUG A   JUG B

RACK PLATE

OCTAGON
RACK PLATE

EGERTON
RACK PLATE

LEEDS SQUARE
FRUIT DISH

LEEDS ROUND
FRUIT DISH

LEEDS OVAL
FRUIT DISH

FRUIT SAUCER

PORRIDGE PLATE

OATMEAL
SAUCER

STAFFORD
DESSERT SET

MASCOT
DESSERT SET

OCTAGON ROUND
FRUIT DISH

OCTAGON
OVAL
FRUIT DISH

OCTAGON
PORRIDGE
PLATE

OCTAGON
OATMEAL
SAUCER

OCTAGON
FRUIT
SAUCER

OCTAGON
SWEET
DISH

MELBOURNE
SANDWICH
TRAY

YORK SANDWICH TRAY

ASTOR CELERY TRAY

BOWLS & TOILET SETS

LENNOX
FLOWER BOWL

REGENT

ALWYN

BULB BOWL

FLOATING FLOWER
BOWL – ROUND

FERN POT
DURHAM

ROUND
SALAD BOWL

QUORN
SALAD BOWL

HECLA
SALAD BOWL

LEITH
SALAD BOWL

CARLTON
BOWL

SPITTOON

MAYFAIR
TOILET SET

LAGOON
TOILET SET

FLAGON
TOILET SET

ALDWYCH
TOILET SET

AUBREY
TOILET SET

ARGOSY
TOILET SET

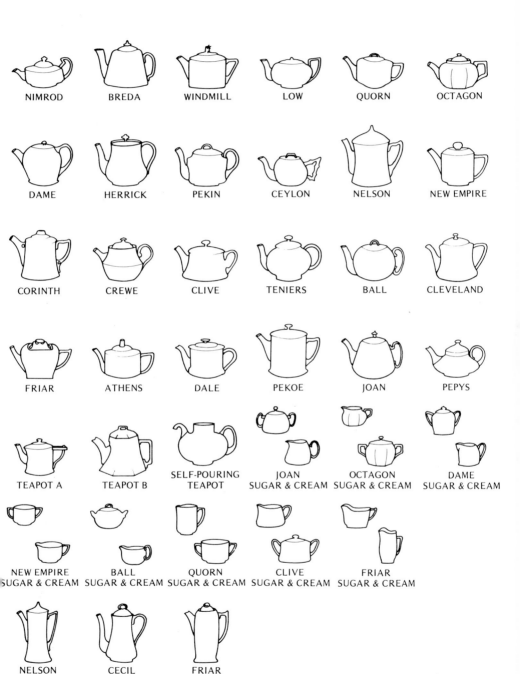

NIMROD · BREDA · WINDMILL · LOW · QUORN · OCTAGON

DAME · HERRICK · PEKIN · CEYLON · NELSON · NEW EMPIRE

CORINTH · CREWE · CLIVE · TENIERS · BALL · CLEVELAND

FRIAR · ATHENS · DALE · PEKOE · JOAN · PEPYS

TEAPOT A · TEAPOT B · SELF-POURING TEAPOT · JOAN SUGAR & CREAM · OCTAGON SUGAR & CREAM · DAME SUGAR & CREAM

NEW EMPIRE SUGAR & CREAM · BALL SUGAR & CREAM · QUORN SUGAR & CREAM · CLIVE SUGAR & CREAM · FRIAR SUGAR & CREAM

NELSON COFFEE POT · CECIL COFFEE POT · FRIAR COFFEE POT

PELICAN
TEACUP
& SAUCER

LINTON
TEACUP
& SAUCER

RHEIMS
TEACUP
& SAUCER

HARLECH
TEACUP
& SAUCER

CECIL
TEACUP
& SAUCER

EMPIRE
TEACUP
& SAUCER

NELSON
TEACUP
& SAUCER

BURKE
BEAKER

STEIN

REX MUG

TRAY

PUFF BOX

PIN TRAY

POMADE
BOX

POWDER
BOX

CANDELSTICKS

PELICAN TRINKET SET

DUTCH
CANDLESTICK

7227
CANDLESTICK

HAIR TIDY

HAT PIN STAND

NEW RIM
ASH TRAY

SAFETY MATCH
STAND

89
ASH TRAY

7710
ASH TRAY

NAPIER
ASH TRAY

CRAIG
ASH TRAY

ANCESTOR
ASH TRAY

89
ASH TRAY

PELICAN
PIN OR ASH TRAY

TOBACCO
JAR

TOBACCO JAR
PATENT CLAMP
FITTING

VIRGINIA
TOBACCO JAR

ASCOT
CHEESE DISH

CHESHIRE
CHEESE DISH

CHEDDAR
CHEESE DISH

CANUTE
CHEESE DISH

MARGOT
BISCUIT BARREL

CECIL
JAM JAR

Index